Nero

IN THE SAME SERIES

General Editors: Eric J. Evans and P.D. King

LANCASTER PAMPHLETS

Nero

David Shotter

London and New York

First published 1997
by Routledge
11 New Fetter Lane, London EC4P 4EE

Simultaneously published in the USA and Canada
by Routledge
29 West 35th Street, New York, NY 10001
© 1997 David Shotter

Typeset in Bembo by
Ponting–Green Publishing Services, Chesham, Buckinghamshire
Printed and bound in Great Britain by
Clays Ltd, St Ives plc

British Library Cataloguing in Publication Data
A catalogue record for this book is available from
the British Library

Library of Congress Cataloguing in Publication Data
Shotter, D. C. A. (David Colin Arthur)
Nero / David Shotter
p.   cm. – (Lancaster pamphlets.)
Includes bibliographical references.
1. Nero, Emperor of Rome, 37–68.
2. Roman Emperors – Biography
3. Rome-History-Nero, 54–68.
I. Title.   II. Series.
DG285. S535   1996
937'.07'092–dc20   96–14839
[B]   CIP

ISBN 0–415–12931–1

Contents

Figures

Foreword

Lancaster Pamphlets offer concise and up-to-date accounts of major historical topics, primarily for the help of students preparing for Advanced Level examinations, though they should also be of value to those pursuing introductory courses in universities and other institutions of higher education. Without being all-embracing, their aims are to bring some of the central themes or problems confronting students and teachers into sharper focus than the textbook writer can hope to do; to provide the reader with some of the results of recent research which the textbook may not embody; and to stimulate thought about the whole interpretation of the topic under discussion.

Acknowledgements

I am grateful to Peter Lee who prepared the maps, which appear as Figures 2–6; to Ghislaine O'Neill for her help in preparing the stemma (Figure 1); and to Susan Waddington for the preparation of the manuscript.

I am grateful to Messrs Aris and Phillips of Warminster for allowing me to reproduce Figures 3–6 from my *Commentary on Suetonius' Lives of Galba, Otho and Vitellius* (1993).

I am also grateful to Penguin Books for permission to reproduce portions from Michael Grant's translation of Tacitus, *Annals* XIV.13, XV.48 and XVI.22 in *Tacitus: The Annals of Imperial Rome*, published in the Penguin Classics series.

Chronology

68	Rebellion of Vindex and Galba; death of Nero (9 June)
69	Rebellions of Vitellius (Germany) and Otho (Rome) against Galba; Galba adopts Piso Licinianus as his successor (12 January); Galba and Piso murdered by the Praetorian Guard and accession of Otho (15 January); defeat at Bedriacum and suicide of Otho (16 April); accession of Vitellius; Vitellius defeated at Bedriacum (October); Antonius Primus enters Rome; Vitellius killed and accession of Vespasian (20 December); Mucianus reaches Rome (end of December)
70	Vespasian and Titus made consuls

1. Stemma of the Julian and Claudian Families

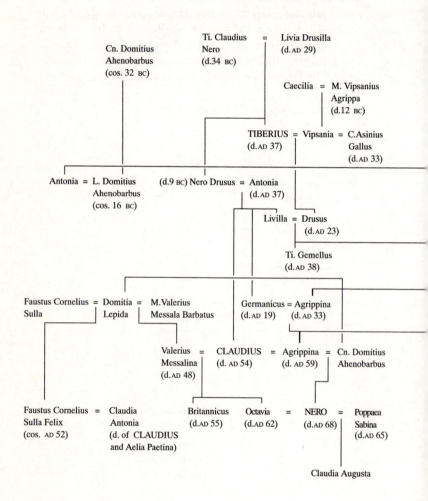

Aurelia = C. Julius Caesar
(d.85 BC)

C. Julius Caesar
(d.44 BC)

Cn. Domitius
Ahenobarbus
(cos. 32 BC)

Ti. Claudius   =   Livia Drusilla
Nero   (d. AD 29)
(d.34 BC)

Caecilia = M. Vipsanius
Agrippa
(d.12 BC)

TIBERIUS = Vipsania = C.Asinius
(d. AD 37)   Gallus
(d. AD 33)

Antonia = L. Domitius   (d.9 BC) Nero Drusus = Antonia
Ahenobarbus   (d. AD 37)
(cos. 16 BC)

Livilla = Drusus
(d. AD 23)

Ti. Gemellus
(d. AD 38)

Faustus Cornelius = Domitia = M.Valerius   Germanicus = Agrippina
Sulla   Lepida   Messala Barbatus   (d. AD 19)   (d. AD 33)

Valerius   =   CLAUDIUS   = Agrippina = Cn. Domitius
Messalina   (d. AD 54)   (d. AD 59)   Ahenobarbus
(d. AD 48)

Faustus Cornelius = Claudia   Britannicus   Octavia = NERO = Poppaea
Sulla Felix   Antonia   (d. AD 55)   (d. AD 62)   (d. AD 68)   Sabina
(cos. AD 52)   (d. of CLAUDIUS   (d. AD 65)
                             and Aelia Paetina)

Claudia Augusta

xiv

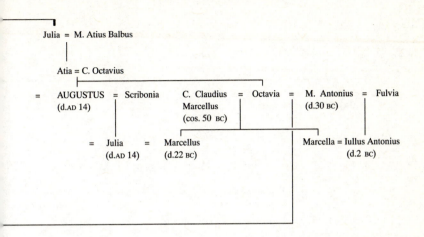

Julia = M. Atius Balbus

Atia = C. Octavius

= AUGUSTUS = Scribonia   C. Claudius = Octavia = M. Antonius = Fulvia
  (d.AD 14)   Marcellus   (d.30 BC)
                   (cos. 50 BC)

= Julia = Marcellus   Marcella = Iullus Antonius
  (d.AD 14)   (d.22 BC)   (d.2 BC)

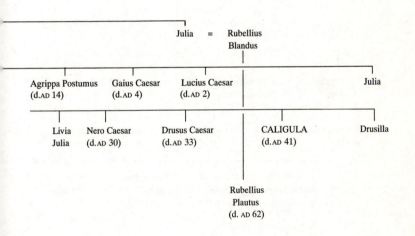

Julia = Rubellius
        Blandus

Agrippa Postumus   Gaius Caesar   Lucius Caesar   Julia
(d.AD 14)   (d.AD 4)   (d.AD 2)

Livia   Nero Caesar   Drusus Caesar   CALIGULA   Drusilla
Julia   (d.AD 30)   (d.AD 33)   (d.AD 41)

Rubellius
Plautus
(d. AD 62)

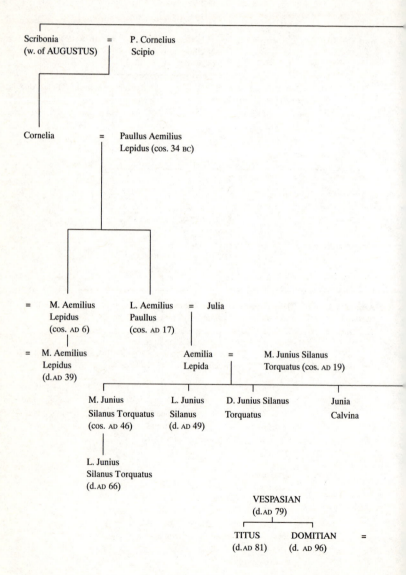

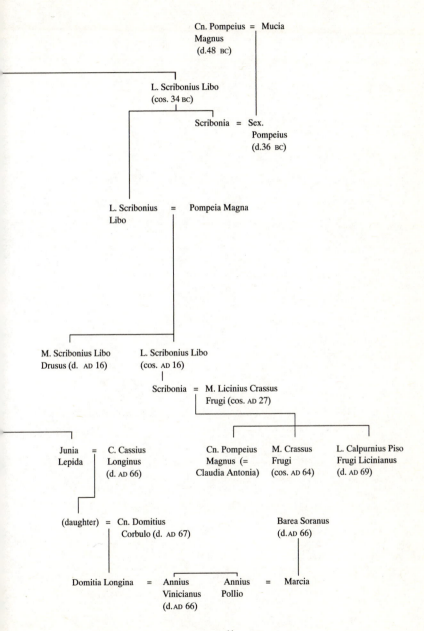

1

Family, politics and early life

Family and politics

The emperor, Nero Claudius Caesar Augustus Germanicus, was the last ruler of the Julio–Claudian dynasty (31 BC–AD 68). His death, precipitated by military rebellion in the western half of the empire, was viewed with great relief by many members of the senatorial order; it demonstrated too that the 'secret of empire was out, that an emperor could be made elsewhere than at Rome' (Tacitus *Histories* I.4) and it prompted some at least to consider alternatives to the concept of dynastic succession (see Appendix 1); Nero, by his behaviour, was seen as hastening the end of the dynasty, but he was viewed more as a product than as the cause of a flawed system.

Dynasticism in Roman politics went back beyond the principate of Augustus; it had been amply demonstrated in the factional manoeuvrings that had characterized the politics of the late republic as groups of nobles joined together to climb the senatorial career ladder (*cursus honorum*) and thereby win honour and glory for themselves and their families. Gradually, however, such ambitions came to appear too self-indulgent, particularly when the factions began to harness elements of the Roman army in their support. This was the route to chaos and civil war, and by the first century BC it was becoming clear to many that the republic needed the guidance of a central ruler;

the real debate surrounded the nature, status and conditions of service of such a person. The crudeness, for example, of the methods of Julius Caesar alienated many amongst the senatorial order; to them, he became a 'king' (*rex*), that most hated figure of Rome's past. Yet many ordinary people valued the strength and apparent security of his patronage; to them, the arrival on the scene of a new Caesar (Octavian – the future emperor, Augustus) was a guarantee of the continuity of what they had come to value in the dictatorship of Caesar (49–44 BC).

Octavian's eventual primacy was guaranteed by his and Agrippa's defeat of Antonius and Cleopatra at the battle of Actium in 31 BC; a war-weary world was not looking for further conflict – rather the stability of a restored republic. Augustus Caesar set about this restoration partly by institutional change and adaptation, and partly by the patronage which his prestige (*auctoritas*) and the wealth of the newly conquered Egypt enabled him to organize. However, in one significant respect there was little real change: the late republic had had only a tenuous institutional control of its army, and it was this that had enabled its incumbent commanders to use the army to further their own ambitions. Although by various reforms Augustus brought to the army a greater measure of stability, he did little to solve the central dilemma; the army under the early principate belonged to the *respublica* only in so far as the emperor was the embodiment of the *respublica*. Thus, while under a strong *princeps* there might appear to be no problem, a weak or uninterested *princeps*, such as Nero seemed to be, demonstrated that control of the army and the hazards which accompanied this were every bit as dangerous to the fabric of the state as during the 'old republic'.

Augustus' personal success depended upon his prestige, his patronage and control, his personality, and his success in tackling some of the problems by which people had been troubled. However just as crucial to his success were the facts that he devised a system of control that suited him and his times, *and that he achieved this gradually*; it is little wonder that the historian Tacitus reflects upon the apparently surreptitious nature of the growth of Augustus' dominance.

However, Augustus' and the republic's real difficulty lay in planning for a future in the longer term, and in devising a scheme which would preclude a return to the extravagances of factional strife which had formerly caused so much trouble. Augustus' preferred solution lay in the construction of a scheme of dynastic succession. The chief difficulty inherent in this or any other scheme was, as Tacitus shows, that the Augustan principate was widely seen as just that, and that people associated peace and stability with Augustus alone; for many, he had after forty-four years assumed a kind of immortality which his ever-youthful appearance on the coinage seemed to confirm.

Augustus had emerged from the battle of Actium as a magistrate with a special mandate; whether this position was to be transmitted, and if so, to whom, were problems to be resolved. It is evident, however, that not everybody believed that Augustus' 'special role' should be extended to someone else after his death; Tacitus reports that, as Augustus' end approached, a few talked of the blessings of *libertas* ('freedom from dominance'), while in the reign of Tiberius (AD 14–37) a historian named Cremutius Cordus was put to death on the grounds that in his *Annals* he had praised Marcus Brutus and dubbed Gaius Cassius 'the last of the Romans' (Tacitus *Annals* I.4, 2; IV.34, 1). Later, in the midst of the civil war which followed Nero's death, his successor, Servius Galba, eloquently put the case for the rejection of a dynastic succession policy in favour of the choice of the best man available (Tacitus *Histories* I.15–16; see Appendix I).

It may be assumed that Augustus' view about the succession had its roots in his own past: although Tacitus specifies an occasion when Augustus discussed the possibility of his powers passing to a man outside his own family, it is clear that his general determination was that he should be succeeded by a member of his own family – the *Julii*, extended by his marriage to Livia into the *Claudii*.

Augustus' extended family had an abundance of potential heirs, but death and intrigue dealt severe blows to his plans for them. Marcellus (his nephew) died in 22 BC, while his stepson, Nero Claudius Drusus, died in 9 BC from complications following a fall. Augustus' adopted sons, Gaius and Lucius Caesar, succumbed respectively in AD 4 and 2; in AD 7 Agrippa Postumus was exiled for an offence, the nature of which it is now hard to unravel. In the meantime, in 6 BC, frustration at the state of his life drove Tiberius (Augustus' other stepson) into retirement on the island of Rhodes; four years later, Tiberius' wife and Augustus' daughter Julia was exiled following the discovery by her father of a host of adulterous relationships with men with very prominent names, including Iullus Antonius, Appius Claudius Pulcher and Tiberius Sempronius Gracchus.

It appeared by AD 4 that a succession policy based upon Augustus' family was near to collapse; in that year the *princeps* adopted Tiberius and Agrippa Postumus jointly as his sons, and required Tiberius to adopt his nephew, Germanicus. Augustus had compromised; while it might no longer be possible for him to be succeeded by a member of the Julian family, he could ensure that his faction would re-emerge in the next generation. The strife between Julians and Claudians appears murderous, but ironically it provided an important ingredient to the success of the Augustan principate for, with two factions – Julians and Claudians – firmly anchored within the system, there was a place in the principate for the factional rivalry which had been an inherent feature of the old republic. Augustus and his Julian family, with its promotion of new families, were the heirs of the *populares* of the republic, while Livia's connections and the sternly traditional outlook of her son Tiberius made him and the Claudian family a natural rallying point for the descendants of the old *optimates*. In this way, it was guaranteed that factional feuding amongst the nobility became part of the principate, rather than continuing on the margins as a danger to the new system.

Tiberius succeeded Augustus in AD 14, and thus Augustus' special mandate had been transmitted to a new generation. The act of transmission, however, conveyed the principate on to new ground; all the powers and honours that Augustus had enjoyed were, despite Tiberius' protests, conveyed to him *en bloc*; he had not, of course, won them, and his title to them came purely by way of the *auctoritas* of Augustus. The *respublica* had become a hereditary monarchy, and in the words of Galba in AD 69, Rome had become the 'heirloom of a single family'. Galba's solution to this situation lay in what Tacitus (*Life of Agricola* 3) referred to as the reconciliation of principate and liberty. As demonstrated in the political fictions of the late first and early second centuries AD this meant that the *princeps* chose as his adopted son and successor the man who by the consensus of his peers in the senate appeared to be the best available. In this way, it seemed, the post of *princeps* effectively became the summit of the senatorial career ladder, and every senator could – in theory at least – aspire to it. As we have seen, there is evidence that at one time Augustus had given thought to this, as Tacitus mentions the names of four such senators who were considered by Augustus as possible successors.

It was believed by some that Augustus would have preferred in AD 14 to have been able to elevate Germanicus Caesar (the son of Nero Drusus) who had married his granddaughter Agrippina. In any event he clearly intended that Germanicus should succeed Tiberius, and required his adoption by Tiberius despite the fact that Tiberius had a son of his own – Drusus – from his first marriage to Vipsania, the daughter of Marcus Agrippa. The evidence suggests that Tiberius intended to honour this requirement, but the plan was dashed by Germanicus' premature death in AD 19.

Germanicus and Agrippina had had three sons – Nero, Drusus and Gaius (Caligula) – and three daughters – Agrippina, Livia and Julia. The elder Agrippina and her older sons (Nero and Drusus) were removed as a result of the intrigues of Lucius Aelius Sejanus, the prefect of the Praetorian Guard, who was himself put to death in AD 31, apparently for plotting the death of the surviving son, Caligula. Of the daughters, Tiberius arranged the marriage of Agrippina to Gnaeus Domitius Ahenobarbus, a man with a good republican pedigree and a poor reputation; these were the parents of the future emperor Nero.

Although Tiberius did not formally adopt a successor, the inevitable choice lay between his natural and adopted grandsons – Tiberius Gemellus and Gaius Caligula. In March of AD 37, Caligula succeeded Tiberius, and within a year Gemellus was dead, possibly as a figurehead of a plot of 'Claudian' senators to remove Caligula. Caligula's interpretation of the principate marked a sharp contrast to those of Augustus and Tiberius; the vigorous pursuit of a personality cult, built around himself and his sisters, who were portrayed in quasi-divine form on the coinage, alienated many. Caligula is said to have encouraged worship of himself as a living god. It is hard to say how far this was true, but the totality of the evidence suggests a monarch whose ideas were absolutist, and who perhaps saw the Hellenistic kings of Asia Minor as his nearest role models.

At first Caligula placed his succession hopes upon his sisters and their husbands, but he was soon disillusioned with them. When he was assassinated in January of AD 41 he left no named heir, and among some of those involved in the plot to kill him there was probably a leaning to a proper return to the republic in preference to a continuation of the principate. However, the Praetorian Guard played its hand, and 'nominated' one of the last surviving members of the Julian and Claudian families, Germanicus' younger brother, Claudius, who may have been involved in his nephew's assassination.

Claudius, because of his family's sense of embarrassment at his physical infirmities, had been kept out of the political limelight for most of his early life until Caligula bestowed upon him a suffect consulship in AD 37. Until then his life had revolved around the study of history from which his own principate was to show that he had gleaned important lessons. In the event, however, the positive aspects of Claudius' thinking were for many (particularly senators) overshadowed by the intrigues and scandals that peppered the reign.

The emperor's third wife, Valeria Messalina, who bore him two children, Britannicus and Octavia, was put to death in AD 48 following her bigamous marriage to a young senator, named Gaius Silius. It may not have been an accident that Silius' father and mother had been close associates of Germanicus and the elder Agrippina, particularly in view of the fact that Messalina's fall opened the way for the younger Agrippina to become Claudius' fourth wife; this marriage took place early in AD 49, and the rise of Agrippina's son achieved real momentum.

Nero's early life and accession

Julia Agrippina was the fourth of the surviving children of Germanicus Caesar and the elder Agrippina, and the eldest of their three daughters; Germanicus' marriage to Agrippina and Augustus' insistence in AD 4 that he be adopted by Tiberius ensured that in the popular mind this family was viewed as representing the true line of descent from Augustus. The younger Agrippina was born on 6 November AD 15, while her parents were on the Rhine, where her father commanded the eight legions of the two Germanies. Tradition has put her birthplace at Cologne, which was later (in AD 50) renamed after her (*Colonia Agrippinensis*).

As we have seen, the family's fortunes during Tiberius' reign seemed to plumb ever-greater depths, with the death of

Germanicus in AD 19 and the attack which was launched in the 20s by Sejanus on the elder Agrippina and her sons. This culminated in their deaths in prison – Nero (the oldest son) in AD 30 or 31 and the elder Agrippina and her second son, Drusus, in AD 33. In the meantime the younger Agrippina was in AD 28 married to Gnaeus Domitius Ahenobarbus (who became consul in AD 32), while in AD 31 Caligula and his two other sisters were taken to reside with Tiberius in his isolated retirement on the island of Capreae. Caligula survived to become *princeps* upon Tiberius' death in AD 37; his youngest sisters were in AD 33 given good marriages – Drusilla to Lucius Cassius Longinus, and Livilla to Marcus Vinicius; these men had shared the consulship of AD 30.

The sisters and their husbands were to play prominent parts in the brief principate of Caligula (AD 37–41). His favourite sister was Drusilla; Gaius had annulled her marriage to Cassius Longinus and married her instead to Marcus Lepidus, a man closer in age to herself. It was upon her that early in AD 38 Gaius indicated that his succession hopes rested; he was devastated by her death in June of that year, and promptly deified her. Indeed a coin of AD 37 showed the three sisters in semi-deified form as 'The Three Graces'. They were made honorary Vestal Virgins, and their names introduced into the imperial oaths. In AD 37 also, Agrippina gave birth to her son, Lucius Domitius Ahenobarbus (later Nero).

The rest of Caligula's short reign was a troubled time for his family; in AD 39 Drusilla's widower, Marcus Lepidus, was put to death on the ground that he was to be the beneficiary of a plot organized by the influential Gnaeus Cornelius Lentulus Gaetulicus, legate of Upper Germany, a man who had been suspected of involvement with Sejanus, but who, against the odds, had survived Sejanus' fall in AD 31.

Agrippina, who was herself widowed in this year, was accused along with her sister, Livilla, of having had an affair with Lepidus, and exiled; her son was deprived of his inheritance, and spent the years of his mother's exile under the protection of Domitia Lepida, his paternal aunt who was herself the mother of Claudius' third wife, Valeria Messalina. Suetonius alleges that Agrippina, even before her husband's death, had been trying to seduce the future emperor Galba.

Claudius' accession in AD 41 led swiftly to the recall from

7

exile of Agrippina and Livilla, both nieces of the new emperor; it was probably at about this time that Agrippina contracted her second marriage – to the wealthy and influential orator and politician, Gaius Sallustius Passienus Crispus, who rose to a second consulship in AD 44. In the meantime, however, probably at the instigation of Messalina, Livilla in AD 42 died in an exile to which she had been consigned as a result of an alleged affair with the stoic philosopher, Lucius Annaeus Seneca. He was also exiled and it is likely that the punishment of this pair should be seen as a sign of Messalina's hostility to the family and friends of Germanicus; Seneca was evidently part of this group – an assertion which appears the more likely in view of Agrippina's influence in having him recalled in AD 49, following her marriage to Claudius.

In AD 47, both Agrippina and her son were the objects of popular enthusiasm when the latter, along with Claudius' son Britannicus, took part in the celebrations of Rome's 800th anniversary; Agrippina and the young Domitius (the future emperor Nero) were now the sole survivors of the family of Germanicus. According to Tacitus, they escaped destruction at the hands of Messalina only because the latter was by now preoccupied with her liaison with Gaius Silius, which led to her death in AD 48.

It cannot be disputed that from Agrippina's point of view the death of Messalina came at a most opportune time. Despite Claudius' stated lack of interest in another marriage, and the existence of other candidates should he change his mind, Agrippina's cause was powerfully promoted. A union between uncle and niece was in Roman law incestuous, but the law was easily surmounted in the interests of the political expediency of conjoining the families of Claudius and Augustus; Claudius had never been adopted into the Julian family and the marriage went some way towards obviating this difficulty. A little before, the engagement of Claudius' daughter Octavia was annulled, and her intended husband, Lucius Junius Silanus, perceived as a natural rival to Domitius in view of Britannicus' youth, was disgraced through the agency of Lucius Vitellius, a member of another family which had been associated with Agrippina's parents. Octavia was now betrothed to Domitius; Silanus committed suicide on the day of Agrippina's marriage to Claudius. At the same time, Seneca's restoration to favour was followed closely by his appointment as Domitius' tutor. Agrippina's successes in AD 49 were crowned by Claudius' adoption (in February) of the young Domitius as his son, now called Nero Claudius Caesar, and later by the conferment upon her of the title Augusta – the first wife of an emperor to receive that name during her husband's lifetime.

In Claudius' last years Agrippina ensured the continuation of her son's advancement: in AD 51 he assumed the toga of manhood (*toga virilis*), though not quite fourteen years of age. It was decided by the senate that a consulate should be reserved for him after his nineteenth birthday (AD 56), that he should enjoy *imperium proconsulare* outside Rome, and that, following in the footsteps of Augustus' adopted sons, Gaius and Lucius Caesar, he should become *princeps iuventutis* (or 'leader of youth'). Nero's status, like that of his mother, found an echo on the contemporary coinage.

By contrast, Claudius' son, Britannicus, was progressively isolated. When Nero appeared at the Games in triumphal robes, Britannicus was still dressed as a boy; indeed, he was not due to receive the toga of manhood until AD 55. Agrippina replaced his tutors with nominees of her own, and, arguing the cause of efficiency, persuaded Claudius to replace the two prefects of the Praetorian Guard, who were thought sympathetic to Britannicus' interests, with a single commander of her choosing – the decent, but pliant, Sextus Afranius Burrus.

Nero's public career also progressed; he made speeches in the senate in AD 51 and 52, the first thanking Claudius for the honours bestowed upon him, the second a vow for the emperor's safe recovery from illness. These were well received, as were petitions he made in AD 53 on behalf of the Italian town of Bononia (Bologna), of Troy, of the island of Rhodes and of the Syrian town of Apamea; the last three speeches were made in Greek, and, whether or not written by Seneca, reflected Nero's early enthusiasm for the culture of the Hellenistic East. In AD 53, Nero married his stepsister, Octavia; she had to be legally transferred to another family to obviate charges of incest.

That Agrippina and her son had a strong following cannot be denied; Agrippina's strength and forcefulness, inherited from her mother, had seen to that – together with the intrigues she had organized against Britannicus. It was likely that Britannicus' assumption of the toga of manhood (on 12 February

AD 55) would be a major test for her, particularly since there were signs, not least perhaps from Claudius himself, that there was support for the young man. Suetonius reports a story that the emperor wished Rome to have a 'real Caesar', and Britannicus enjoyed the strong support of Claudius' loyal and influential freedman (*libertus*), Narcissus. The senate's expulsion of Tarquitius Priscus in AD 53 showed its readiness to attack a friend of Agrippina; further, the disposal of Domitia Lepida, her own sister-in-law but perhaps more importantly Britannicus' grandmother, may be taken as an attempt on her part to undermine him. To such evidence may be added – if they are not just examples of provincial ignorance – coins from Moesia and North Africa placing Britannicus' head and title on the obverse side.

The death of Claudius in October AD 54 was ascribed by most ancient authors to poison administered at the behest of Agrippina, who presumably both feared the possible resurgence of an interest in Britannicus and felt that she had done enough to prepare for Nero's elevation; Josephus is the only historian who admitted the story to be only a rumour. It has been pointed out that the supposition that mushrooms were responsible derived from Nero's quip about mushrooms being the food of gods. However, mistakes can be made with poisonous fungi, so that a venomous item could have escaped the food-taster, whose corruption does not therefore have to be assumed in this instance.

Agrippina was every bit as conscious of the needs of security as Livia appears to have been in AD 14 when her son Tiberius succeeded Augustus; no opportunity was offered for the causes of Britannicus and Octavia to be espoused. Nero was presented by Burrus to the Praetorian Guard, to each member of which was promised a substantial donative for hailing the seventeen-year-old as *imperator*. Britannicus was kept indoors and, according to Tacitus, those few soldiers who asked about him were favoured with no reply. Claudius' will was suppressed, which is generally taken to indicate that it favoured Britannicus.

The success of Agrippina's crusade on her son's behalf cannot be denied; single-minded and determined, she fully deserves the observation made about her by Tacitus at the time of her marriage to Claudius:

10

From this moment the country was transformed. Complete obedience was accorded to a woman – and not a woman like Messalina who toyed with national affairs. This was a rigorous, almost masculine, despotism. In public, Agrippina was austere and often arrogant. Her private life was chaste – unless power was to be gained. Her passion to acquire money was unbounded; she wanted it as a stepping-stone to supremacy.

Elsewhere, she is characterized by the historian as 'a relentless enemy'. If she needed such characteristics as Tacitus describes to bring her son to power, she needed them no less if she was to maintain her dominance over him once he had become emperor. 'The best of mothers' – as Nero described her in his opening watchword to the guard – was in the last months of AD 54 facing her greatest test.

In the opening months of the reign, honours were accorded to Agrippina well in excess of those that had previously been used to show favour to women of the imperial family – certainly during their lifetimes. She was given an official escort as if she were a magistrate, and Nero had the senate meet in his residence so that Agrippina could listen in. He publicly paraded his dutiful affection, and into AD 55 her head and titles appeared on the coinage, first in a dominant postion and then alongside those of her son. After Claudius' deification his widow was made a priestess of the new cult.

Yet it has been observed that Tacitus is careful to emphasize the *public* nature of this attention as if, in his view, it was really a façade. Although it was Agrippina who had brought in Seneca as a tutor to her son, the ideas on government as expressed in the Senecan oration delivered by Nero to the senate at his accession contained themes which will not have given Agrippina much comfort, as both explicitly and implicitly they denied the methods of government that characterized the years in which she had been Claudius' consort. Particularly worrying was the fact that the Neronian/Senecan criticism of the role of freedmen in the government was followed in AD 55 by Nero's dismissal of Pallas, the financial aide, to whom of all Claudius' freedmen Agrippina was closest. Nor will she have been happy at the degree to which Seneca and Burrus, her protégé who was prefect of the Praetorian Guard, demonstrated their independence of

11

her. There is in Agrippina's behaviour an echo of the sense of persecution that had characterized her mother's behaviour in widowhood. What Seneca and Burrus probably saw as relatively harmless in Nero – his cultural pursuits and his affair with the slave-girl Acte – were to her signs of her son's dangerous emancipation of himself from her influence.

In such circumstances, her countermove was exceedingly ill-judged: she attempted to bring Nero back into line by threatening to champion the cause of Britannicus. Claudius' natural and adopted sons had never enjoyed a good relationship; Britannicus' criticism of Nero's singing voice and his reference to his adoptive brother by his original name of Lucius Domitius can hardly have been harmless banter. The young man, described pointedly by Tacitus as 'the last of the Claudians', was poisoned in the palace; it is a sign of the marginalization of both Britannicus and Agrippina that the deed appears to have caused little general anxiety. Ominously for Agrippina, neither Seneca nor Burrus complained: either they had been bought off or, regarding Britannicus' death as inevitable given the young man's relationship with Nero, they simply decided to concentrate on matters concerning their influence with Nero which in the longer run they saw as more significant.

Angry recriminations between mother and son led to her expulsion from the imperial presence, and to her ill-judged fostering of other friendships designed to aggravate her son: these involved Octavia, the estranged wife of the *princeps* and, according to an accusation brought against her, Rubellius Plautus, the great-grandson of Tiberius, who was thus connected to Augustus in a manner not unlike Nero himself. It was, however, a sign of the realization on the part of Seneca and Burrus that they could not dispense with Agrippina that they managed to cool Nero's hostility towards his mother, though it would appear that they achieved this only at the price of weakening their own influence with him. There are indications of a growing lack of trust in them on the emperor's part and of a more decisive emancipation from the standards of conduct which they had attempted to set for him.

Increasingly Nero identified his mother as the one principally determined to check his pleasures and to interfere in his life. Things took a far more serious turn when, probably in AD 58, Nero began his love affair with Poppaea Sabina, a lady whose noble lineage and expectations were in a class very different from those of Acte. It was Agrippina's opposition to this, and Nero's determined desire to be free to 'lead his own life', that convinced him that his only solution was to rid himself permanently of his mother. In an official version, which was supported subsequently by Seneca and Burrus, Nero claimed that his mother had plotted his assassination. In truth her murder by Anicetus, the prefect of the fleet at Misenum, was the bizarre culmination of a bizarre plot thought up by Nero himself. Seneca and Burrus may not have approved of the deed, but again they trimmed by supporting the official version in an effort to retain their influence over their now wayward pupil.

Many people may have found Agrippina overbearing, as she certainly was to Nero; she was ruthless in her pursuit of ambition, as many who found themselves in her way discovered. But she still had friends in high places who, while they may have accommodated themselves to the needs of the moment, entertained a residual respect for the house of Germanicus and for a connection with Augustus which Agrippina's son hardly seemed to embody. In any case, freed from his mother's domination, Nero now considered others, who may previously have seemed the lesser of evils, irksome in their wish to keep him on a track of their choice; thus the influence of Seneca and Burrus was immeasurably weakened by the fall of Agrippina and the rise of Poppaea Sabina. Many more who remembered the emphasis placed by Augustus on the Roman family and the mother's pivotal, even sacred, role within it will have been shattered by this blow; the death of Nero's mother was to return to haunt the *princeps*.

2

The new Augustus

Nero came to power in AD 54 amid general hopes and expectations; in the short term – outwardly, at least – he was not to disappoint. To distinguish this promising start from the evident deterioration of later years, many modern writers have applied to the first five years of Nero's reign (AD 54–58) the term *quinquennium Neronis*: according to the fourth-century historian, Aurelius Victor, this term had been used of Nero by Trajan (AD 98–117), although it seems likely that by it Trajan was alluding with approval to the building activities of Nero's final five years.

However, Tacitus too appears to have marked a change in Nero's government after the first five years, for he prefaces his account of AD 59 with the words: 'Nero ceased delaying his long-meditated crime' (that is, the murder of his mother). Moreover, he closes his account of the previous year with the omen of impending doom considered to have been represented by the withering of the ancient fig tree, the *ficus Ruminalis*; the tree's revival, with new shoots, was deemed to be equally unsettling. Also significant for Tacitus' attitude is the *structural* evidence of his *Annals*. In his account of Tiberius' reign (*Annals* I–VI), the historian adhered closely to an annalistic framework, narrating events strictly within the context of the years to which they belonged, with the opening and closing of books coinciding with the beginnings and ends of years. In what survives of the later books of the *Annals* this happens more rarely, although the strict adherence to the framework is conspicuously present in *Annals* XIII, which covers events from Nero's accession up to the end of AD 58. This appears to suggest that Tacitus saw this time as a significant turning point in the character of Nero's government.

Without doubt, Agrippina's murder in AD 59 was an horrendous act, which in the eyes of many damaged Nero's reputation totally and forever. Yet in *some* other respects, the year appears less significant; the influence of Seneca and Burrus continued for three more years, and the emperor's tolerable relations with the senate survived as well. Equally it would be unwise to attach an unblemished character to everything that happened before AD 59; Tacitus' introduction to *Annals* XIV (cited above) implies a degree of hypocrisy in Nero's earlier behaviour. As we saw in the last chapter, this earlier period included the murder of Britannicus and attacks on others who were considered a threat to the regime.

Of significance to the character of the government in Nero's earlier years were the youth and character of the *princeps* which gave him an 'alternative agenda' of self-indulgence; further, the continuing influence of Agrippina (for a while, at least) and of Seneca and Burrus ensured that more experienced hands were at the government's disposal.

In his youth Nero had been given a variety of mentors in rhetoric and philosophy; he also cultivated an interest in a wide range of 'artistic' subjects, such as art, architecture and music. However, Seneca, who had been born at Cordoba in Spain but educated in Rome, was the most significant of his tutors. His task had been to educate his young charge in rhetoric and philosophy although, like many Roman parents at this time, Agrippina took care to ensure that her son did not become too involved in philosophy. Seneca was wealthy and worldly, and it is clear from his philosophical treatises, such as *On Clemency* (*De Clementia*), that his stoicism did not give Nero access to the strident 'republicanism' that is sometimes associated with members of the sect in the later first century AD, but will have sought to inculcate into him the attributes of the good ruler, which was one of the commonplaces of stoic philosophy; the speech which Seneca wrote for Nero to deliver in the senate at the time of his accession was redolent with such ideas. Burrus, on the other hand, who was a native of Vaison in Provence, was not an intellectual or a high flier but was seen as a sound administrator and a man of integrity. He was the perfect associate of the affable and worldly Seneca, and Tacitus recognized in their partnership a unanimity rare for men in such powerful positions.

Nero's role models were Claudius and Augustus, the two predecessors who received the posthumous honour of deification. These were significant for different reasons; the enthusiasm of many provincial communities for Claudius' fair and often generous treatment of them made it essential that, for them at least, Nero be seen as the active promoter of such policies. The fact that Nero was the former emperor's adopted son appeared to lend substance to such a hope; in any case, as a provincial himself Seneca had a natural interest in the promotion of policies designed to enhance the status and well-being of the provinces. A papyrus from Egypt (*Oxyrhynchus Papyrus* 1021), dated 17 November AD 54, encapsulated the hope:

> The Caesar who has honoured his debt to his ancestors, who is a god manifest, has gone to them; the expectation and hope of all the world has been proclaimed Emperor; the good genius of the world and the beginning of all great and good things, Nero, has been proclaimed Caesar. So wearing garlands and making sacrifice of oxen we must all pay our thanks to all the Gods. Issued in the 1st year of Nero Claudius Caesar Augustus Germanicus, on the 21st of the month Neos Sebastos.

Taking up the current mood, two of the voting tribes of the city of Alexandria renamed themselves *Philoclaudios* (indicating Nero's affection for his adoptive father), and *Propapposebasteios* (recalling the new emperor's great-great-grandfather, Augustus).

In Rome, however, Claudius' memory was differently assessed: Claudius' name retained a reference in Nero's official nomenclature, but greater emphasis was given to the maternal line, which connected Nero with the deified Augustus:

> Nero Claudius Caesar Augustus Germanicus, son of the Deified Claudius, grandson of Germanicus Caesar, great-grandson of Tiberius Caesar Augustus, great-great-grandson of the Deified Augustus.

Although Nero's early coins mentioned Claudius' name in the titulature, this did not last beyond AD 56, and in any case never appeared on the bronze coinage (small change) at all. The reason is not far to seek; the deification of Claudius may have been desired by Agrippina but was principally a useful way of stressing imperial continuity and of giving Nero the opportunity to display – and presumably gain credit for – a show of filial devotion (*pietas*) similar to that which Augustus had shown to Julius Caesar, and Tiberius to the deified Augustus.

The true feeling of the new government for the old, however, emerges dramatically in Seneca's hard-hitting satire on Claudius' deification – the *Apocolocyntosis* (or 'Pumpkinification'). This catalogued Claudius' failings clearly and demonstrated the basis of his unpopularity; little doubt could be left that the new government did not see a model for its own conduct in that of Claudius.

Nero's own first public statements revealed clear criticisms of Claudius' methods of government; in a speech written for him by Seneca, Nero rejected various items of Claudian practice and undertook a return to more traditional (that is, Augustan) ways. He promised to honour the senate's integrity, to abolish trials for treason (*maiestas*) and proceedings heard privately by the *princeps*. He also promised that he would remove freedmen from the positions of power that they had held under Claudius; the removal of Agrippina's favourite, Pallas, within months of the accession served to show that Nero meant what he said, though his motive, as we saw in the previous chapter, probably had little to do with conciliating the senate.

The coinage too bore signs of the new policy; a coin of AD 55, which bore Agrippina's legend on the obverse, showed an elephant-drawn chariot (*quadriga*) containing the figures of Divus Claudius and Divus Augustus, the latter of which was clearly more prominent. The context recalls the severe criticisms of Claudius uttered by Divus Augustus in Seneca's *Apocolocyntosis*. Unusually, *ex S C* ('by decree of the senate') appeared on the gold and silver coinage rather than simply on bronze issues, and a common device on the early gold and silver was the oak-wreath crown, which will have recalled Augustus' use of this containing the legend, *OB CIVES SERVATOS* ('for having saved the citizens').

In his earlier years at least, Nero's government displayed a tendency in appointments to the consulship to favour men whose families had been raised to senatorial status by Augustus, and even those descended from republican nobility; in each of the first six years of the reign (AD 55–60), although Nero himself held a consulship in four of these, at least one of the *ordinarii* was of late republican nobility – Lucius Antistius Vetus (55), Publius Cornelius Scipio (56), Lucius Calpurnius Piso (57), Marcus Valerius Messala Corvinus (58), Gaius Fonteius Capito (59), Cossus Cornelius Lentulus (60). Subsequently this tendency diminished although, like Augustus, after his early consulships Nero refused a permanent consulship (or a 'reserved' annual place), and after AD 60 held the office only once more – as a suffect during the confused events of the summer of AD 68.

Ever since Augustus' times, there had been, as Tacitus noted, a growing tendency on the senate's part to indulge in empty flattery and it showed an unwillingness to take decisions that might run counter to the wishes of the *princeps*. Although such tendencies continued in Nero's reign, there are clear signs in the earlier years at least of a general contentment among senators.

Outwardly at least, Nero's government seemed moderate and conciliatory; although the new *princeps* took most of his powers *en bloc* at the beginning of his reign, he initially (until AD 56) refused the title of *pater patriae* ('father of his country'). This approach seems to have recalled the reserve shown by Tiberius over the imperial titulature, particularly the name *Augustus*, and the title *pater patriae*. Both Nero and Tiberius may have had in mind the 'gradualist' approach of Augustus in their anxiety to recapture a successful formula. Nero rejected extravagant honours – the proposals that his birth-month (December) should become the beginning of the year, the suggestion that statues of the new emperor in silver and gold should be erected in public, and (as we have seen) the proposal that he should take on a permanent consulship.

Nero's attitude to the senate and to senators was constructive; he avoided imposing crippling burdens and (much to Agrippina's annoyance) he cancelled the requirement, introduced by Claudius, that quaestors-designate – that is, young men in their early twenties – should stage gladiatorial shows. He continued the practice of his predecessors of offering financial help to senators who had fallen on hard times, so that they would not have to forfeit senatorial status. In AD 55 he even excused his

18

consular colleagues the normal obligation of swearing to uphold the emperor's enactments.

The senate's business in these years followed traditional Augustan lines, demonstrating co-operation between itself and the *princeps* over a range of social issues, particularly regarding slaves and ex-slaves, and matters pertaining to the security and well-being of Italy, which was beginning to show signs of social and economic stress by the middle of the first century AD. Port-facilities were enhanced at a number of places, especially along the west coast – for example, at Ostia, Antium (Anzio), Puteoli (Pozzuoli) and Tarentum (Taranto). Depopulation was becoming a problem as veteran legionaries, who had been recruited largely in Italy, increasingly chose to settle in retirement in the provinces in which they had served. This was checked by a programme of *colonia*-foundation in Italy, as at Pompeii and Puteoli.

Law and order was also becoming a difficulty; *princeps* and senate co-operated closely in an effort to handle disturbances which had broken out at Puteoli because of suspected corruption among local officials. At Pompeii in AD 59, an outbreak of strife and hooliganism which had disfigured a performance at the amphitheatre led to a ten-year closure of the building as a punitive and preventative measure. The foundation of a *colonia* there was probably either precipitated by this or intended to reinvigorate the town after a disastrous earthquake in AD 63, the results of which can still be seen in the patching of buildings which remained unfinished at the time of the catastrophic eruption of Vesuvius in AD 79. Such concern for Italy will have been welcome to senators, and was clearly intended as a move to redress the imbalance which was perceived to be the result of Claudius' great enthusiasm for provincial advancement. Nonetheless, as we shall see, Nero's government continued the process of provincial enhancement. As prosperity and the Roman citizenship spread, so too did the ability of men from further afield to win advancement to higher positions. Nero's favour, particularly in the early years, towards senators of republican and Augustan origins was probably an attempt to reassure Romans and Italians that they would not be outstripped by such new developments; Tacitus shows that Claudius' radicalism over senatorial membership had caused traditionalists real anxiety.

A similar emphasis is also found in Nero's early handling of judicial and financial matters. He certainly avoided the highly unpopular Claudian practice of hearing cases in private. Suetonius attests that Nero characteristically took considerable care in the hearing of cases, and ensured that his own judgements were based on the *written* opinions of his assessors. His own decisions were likewise published in writing. This suggests an anxiety on the part of the government to be fair and clear, and in these respects early Neronian practices probably betray the hands of Seneca and Burrus.

His financial management was also generally sound, although detail is now hard to reconstruct, particularly since it is virtually impossible to distinguish between the activities of the state's various treasuries. Like his predecessors, Nero certainly made gifts to the main treasury (*aerarium Saturni*) from his private fortune, which was kept large through the legacies and bequests that were made to him. The dismissal of Claudius' financial agent Pallas certainly led to more open administration, and greater efficiency was evidently the aim of replacing the quaestors who were nominally in charge with two prefects of his own choosing from men of praetorian standing.

One of Nero's most interesting financial initiatives, however, was not brought to fruition. In AD 58 he suggested the abolition of indirect taxation (*vectigalia*) across the empire. At its simplest, this may have been no more than a radical attempt to rein in the activities of the tax gatherers (*publicani*). These men, highly unscrupulous and unpopular during the republic, had been brought under a far greater measure of state control by Augustus, but still inflicted hardship by their greed and corruption – as Tacitus makes clear in a brief account of tax irregularities in Britain which were eventually curtailed by Agricola. Indeed, four years later (in AD 62), Nero established a commission of three ex-consuls to examine a range of financial matters, particularly the collection of indirect taxes, apparently because he wanted a far greater degree of order in the state's financial transactions.

It is, however, possible that Nero – under the influence of Seneca and Burrus – had a more exciting aim in mind: the removal of indirect taxation would have accelerated the growth of trade and thus the ability of individuals across the empire to enhance their wealth. The state would not have lost, because the missing taxation would have been replaced by a correspondingly greater yield from direct taxation. Further, the enhancement of personal wealth would have led to a greater opportunity for provincials to participate in public careers at local level, for which wealth was an essential qualification. The idea was eventually dropped; it would possibly have been impracticable, but it accords well with the broadly-based wish of the new government to achieve equity in its treatment of *all* the empire's subjects.

It is, of course, not possible to determine how far this high standard of administration occurred because of, or in spite of, Nero. Were these the ideas essentially of Seneca and Burrus filling a vacuum left by a young *princeps* whose mind was largely directed towards personal pleasure? Or did that young *princeps* have ideas of his own?

The answer may be beyond us, but it is important to balance our view of the generally high standard of administration characteristic of the earlier years of Nero's government with an account of his personal conduct and of the intrigues of the court during this same period. For an emperor devoted to pursuing his own agenda, and basking in the apparently uncritical popularity showered upon him by the senate and those around him, there had to come a point at which that private agenda would impinge more harshly on the affairs of state. It is, however, a testament to the success of the public relations conducted by and for him during those early years that his popularity could survive not just dynastic intrigues but even, apparently, an act as naturally repulsive to Roman sentiment as matricide.

As we have seen, Tacitus represents this act as a major turning point in the reign. It is obvious that as Nero grew older he came to resent his mother's attempts to dominate him – to the extent that on one occasion he even threatened to abdicate. Without Agrippina's ever-watchful eye, Nero was obviously able with less constraint to follow his social and artistic pleasures.

Agrippina's murder was both horrendous in principle and bizarre in execution, but what precisely lay behind it is less clear. It has been shown that all the basic questions which arise from an effort to explain the event are hard to answer because of a complex set of inconsistencies in the surviving sources. One version holds that Nero fell in love early on with Poppaea Sabina while she was married to Rufrius Crispinus, Claudius' prefect of the Praetorian Guard who was removed from his command in AD 51 at Agrippina's instigation, and that he used his friend, Marcus Salvius Otho (the future emperor), as a 'cover' for his relationship with Poppaea and to keep it from Agrippina. Otho became over-involved with Poppaea, and was 'protected' by Seneca who had him sent in AD 58 to be governor of Lusitania (Portugal). In this version of events, it was then Poppaea who urged Nero to kill his mother as the obstacle which stood between them.

However, other versions plainly existed; indeed five different stories of Nero's affair with Poppaea have been recognized in the sources – Tacitus himself subscribing to two in different places! It is clear simply from the chronology that Agrippina's death did not precipitate Nero's marriage to Poppaea. His divorce from Octavia did not occur until AD 62, after the death of Burrus, a supporter of Octavia and a firm opponent of the divorce. It is indeed possible that Nero did not become involved with Poppaea until AD 62, and that the whole episode has been placed earlier by sources no longer extant in order to use it as the explanation of the matricide. The reason for Agrippina's murder probably lay in the complex relationship which she enjoyed with her son. Paradoxically, Nero both needed and resented her domination of him. Her murder was his means of escape, though it has been suggested that the fact his second and third marriages (to Poppaea Sabina and to Statilia Messalina) were to women older than himself demonstrated his need to be dominated by a mother-figure.

Seneca and Burrus probably did not approve of the deed, and Burrus was on record as having indicated that the praetorians would not become involved in it. However, they had already demonstrated at the beginning of the reign that Nero was their primary concern, and they had played their parts in the marginalizing of Agrippina. So now they probably went along with a damage-limitation exercise, in which Burrus kept the praetorians loyal to Nero, while Seneca composed a letter in which Nero sought to justify his act by claiming that Agrippina bore the responsibility for all the unsavoury practices of Claudius' reign and that she had been caught trying to organize Nero's assassination. Such was Nero's popularity in the senate and Seneca's success in his justification that Nero won the senate's approval for what he had done; only one senator, the stoic Thrasea

Paetus, refused to acquiesce. Agrippina, despite her lineage, had few real friends.

In AD 62 Burrus died; according to Tacitus, this broke the power of Seneca, who was granted leave to retire. It is unlikely that Seneca, by now aged sixty-five, would have wished to carry on by himself – or indeed thought himself capable of it. Equally, it is unlikely that Nero now felt any need of tutors and minders. In the command of the Praetorian Guard Nero returned to dualism – appointing the pliant Faenius Rufus, who was reckoned to have been an effective manager of the corn supply, and the vicious Ofonius Tigellinus who saw it as his function to pander to all of Nero's worst instincts.

Burrus had consistently opposed the divorce from Octavia, and it is apparent that his death now cleared the way for this; his objection had been that Nero's marriage to Claudius' daughter was an essential element of his title to be Claudius' successor. Consequently for Nero the prospect of his divorce raised the spectre of rivals, and it was presumably because of this that, after Burrus' death, Tigellinus persuaded Nero to sanction the deaths of both Rubellius Plautus and Faustus Sulla, on the ground that these men, with their connections with the imperial house, could provide the rivalry that Nero feared. Both had previously been excluded from Rome – respectively to Marseilles and Asia.

The stated ground for divorce was that Octavia had produced no heir for Nero. The generous initial settlement indicates how anxious Nero was concerning the popularity of Octavia – the one member of the imperial family who was reputed to be above corruption and malice. Nero's marriage to Poppaea Sabina soon followed, and the consequent demonstrations in favour of Octavia provided an indication of popular feeling. That Poppaea and especially Nero felt under threat is hardly surprising. The consequences of such fears, however, were harsh: Octavia's terms of banishment were toughened and allegations made that she was involved with Anicetus, prefect of the fleet and murderer of Agrippina. On 9 June AD 62, she was put to death on orders from Rome.

Thus in three years Nero had lost the four most significant restraints upon him – Agrippina, Octavia, Seneca and Burrus. He survived the reactions to these losses and was now free to pursue his own path, from which respect for these people and their popular followings had earlier restrained him. The reputation he had gained from a studious observance of Augustus' principles in government ironically now left him with a sufficiently strong power-base from which to launch a new agenda for government. This was far removed from those of both Claudius and Augustus.

3

Empire and provinces

Nero is (and was) regarded as one of the most unmilitary of emperors; his lack of interest in his armies contributed in no small way to his downfall in AD 68. Yet Nero's armies were involved in more warfare than was often the case, and the Elder Pliny suggests that expeditions were planned into Ethiopia (modern Sudan) and the Caucasus region, although in the event these never took place. Nevertheless it is worth pointing out that, at least until his later years, Nero felt sufficiently strong and secure to appoint commanders who were of high calibre and reputation – men such as Suetonius Paullinus (Britain) and Domitius Corbulo (in the east).

In Europe, the frontier of the empire's territory had since the beginning of the reign of Tiberius been formed by the Rhine and Danube rivers; there was no longer any overt ambition to push the Rhine frontier further eastwards. The 'two Germanies' – Upper (*Superior*) in the south, and Lower (*Inferior*) in the north – were, until the time of Domitian in the late first century AD, military zones rather than provinces. They comprised territory on the west bank of the Rhine with frontier structures enhancing the defensive role of the river itself. In addition, some land was held on the east bank and used for 'support services'.

The Rhine was a significant frontier area; the Romans entertained a healthy respect for those who lived beyond it. The Cimbri and the Teutones had, in the late second century BC,

25

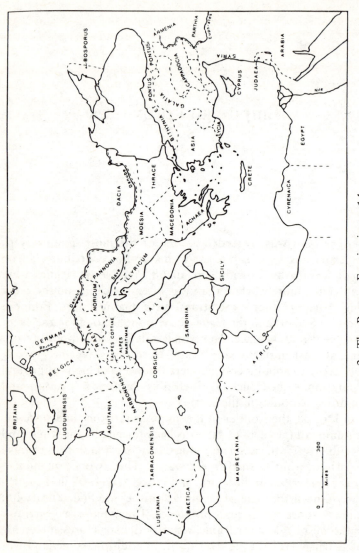

2. The Roman Empire in AD 14

migrated through western Europe and had been driven from Italy only through the victories of Gaius Marius. Julius Caesar's extended proconsulship of Gaul in the fifties BC had been occasioned by the crossing to the west bank of the Rhine by the tribal leader, Ariovistus, and by his harassment of Gallic tribes who lived there.

Augustus brought enhanced order to the area, which depended upon his positioning of eight legions in permanent fortresses along the Rhine. His push for the Elbe, however, was effectively terminated by the disaster in AD 9, which resulted in the total loss of three legions (XVII, XVIII and XIX) at the hands of the Cheruscan chieftain Arminius who, like a number of local leaders in the Augustan and later periods, appeared 'safe' because of a veneer of Romanization. The search for the Elbe frontier was finally called off in AD 16 when Tiberius recalled Germanicus, after the latter had come close to being embroiled in a fiasco similar to that of AD 9.

It is not surprising in view of the setbacks and disasters that had been suffered in the area that the Romans felt a sensitivity and anxiety over the tribes who occupied land between the Rhine and the Elbe. Roman writers shared a preoccupation with this area. In the reign of Vespasian (AD 69–79), the Elder Pliny wrote his definitive *German Wars*, while twenty years later the historian Tacitus wrote a treatise on the German tribes, which we know as the *Germania*. The Elder Seneca preserved a vivid passage on the near-disaster of Germanicus' campaign of AD 15, written in verse by one of Germanicus' officers, Albinovanus Pedo. Such writings appear to have carried an implicit warning to Romans of the dangers that lurked beyond (and sometimes also on the Roman side of) the Rhine – dangers that might conceivably threaten even the territorial integrity of Italy.

During Nero's reign, the Younger Seneca wrote of the fearsome martial prowess and toughness of German tribesmen. This was presumably prompted by disturbances in Lower Germany among tribes of the east bank; these were caused probably by land shortage, but the consequent political instability of these tribes was prevented from developing into serious outbreaks by military threats from the governors of the Germanies and by the habitual inability of the tribes to co-operate with each other.

Clearly a part of the longer-term solution to such problems was to draw German tribesmen on to the Roman side – by grants of citizenship to individual leaders, and by recruiting Germans into auxiliary units of the Roman army (such as the ten thousand members of the Batavian cohorts), and into the *classis Germanica*, the fleet which patrolled the Rhine. That such a policy could still carry risks, however, is shown by the Gallo-German rising in AD 69 under Julius Civilis and Julius Classicus.

Under Claudius and Nero, seven legions were stationed on the Rhine; in Lower Germany, there were two (V *Alaudae* and XV *Primigenia*) at Vetera (Xanten), and one each (respectively XVI *Gallica* and I *Germanica*) at Novaesium (Neuss) and Bonna (Bonn). Three legions held Upper Germany – IV *Macedonica* and XXII *Primigenia* at Moguntiacum (Mainz) and XXI *Rapax* at Vindonissa (Windisch). Under the later Julio–Claudians, programmes were in place for replacing earlier turf-and-timber structures with stone and brick, and for providing in an organized fashion outside the fortresses a range of support services that the legions required. At intervals between the fortresses were smaller forts for auxiliary troops; the evidence for the Julio–Claudian period is that the bulk of these were situated on the west bank of the river. The highly complex arrangements of forts, watchtowers, roads and palisades on the eastern bank south of Mainz, forming the *limes Germanicus* and the *limes Raeticus*, were largely the creation of the Flavian and later emperors. Of Neronian date, however, was the completion on the west bank in Lower Germany of an embankment, which had been started by Nero's great-grandfather, Nero Claudius Drusus.

In Nero's time, the Danube was not held with the strength later associated with this frontier; the long stretch from Vindonissa (Windisch) to Carnuntum (a little downstream of Vienna) had no legion, but was protected by the provinces of Raetia and Noricum, whose governors were equestrians rather than senators and who had not had any troops under their command until Claudius' time. The reason for this was that the tribe of the Marcomanni (of modern Bohemia), which had proved so formidable a strength in Augustus' time, was at this stage in eclipse. Pannonia had one legion (XV *Apollinaris*, later replaced by X *Gemina*) on the river at Carnuntum, while the province's other legion (XIII *Gemina*) was well inland at Poetovio (Pettau). There was also one legion (XI *Pia Fidelis*) at Burnum (Kistanje) in Dalmatia. Along the Lower Danube, the

province of Moesia had three legions – VII *Claudia Pia Fidelis*
at Viminacium (Kostolac), V *Macedonica* (and later III *Gallica*)
at Oescus (Gigen) and VIII *Augusta* at Novae (Svistow).

It was only in the later Julio–Claudian period that the security
of territory on the northern bank of the Danube began to come
into question. In the late fifties and early sixties there is evidence
of westward movement by tribes such as the Alani, Roxolani,
Sarmatians and Dacians, who were to prove so troublesome
later in the century. Such movements were caused presumably
by population pressure from further east; on this occasion, the
problem was solved, temporarily at least, by the decision of
Plautius Silvanus (governor of Moesia) to resettle one hundred
thousand of these tribesmen on the Roman side of the river.
Nonetheless, it is significant that by the time of the Year of the
Four Emperors (AD 69) pressure was building anew.

In the west Nero's most difficult problems occurred in Britain.
Since the invasion of AD 43 conquest had been pursued logically
northwards and westwards. Treaties kept some part of the
island under pro-Roman monarchs; part of the territory of the
Atrebates (in Hampshire and Sussex) was left in the hands of
Cogidubnus with a new tribal name of Regni (or Regnenses),
the 'territory of the king'. The northern parts of East Anglia,
which on the evidence of pre-Roman artefacts was a very
wealthy area, were left under the control of Prasutagus, while
the tribe of the Brigantes, whose territory covered all of northern England, enjoyed a treaty under their queen, Cartimandua.
In the mid-Neronian years, under the governor Suetonius Paullinus, the chief objective was the reduction of north Wales and,
in particular, the rooting out of the centres of Druidic power on
the island of Mona (Anglesey).

To the rear, those parts of the province that had been subdued
early on were beginning to adapt to Roman government and
culture; this process was centred on the new *colonia* founded in
AD 49 at Camulodunum (Colchester), previously the centre of
the tribes of the Catuvellauni and Trinovantes. As a result of the
foundation of the *colonia* there were tensions over land con-
fiscation for the veteran settlers and, according to Tacitus,
particularly over the decision to establish on a large site in the
colonia a substantial temple of the imperial cult – regarded as a
'symbol of the alien domination', for which both local land and
money were appropriated.

Worse was to come; in AD 59, Prasutagus, the client-king of the Iceni, died. Since his treaty arrangement was one agreed on a personal basis with Claudius, it was always unlikely that it would be allowed to continue after his death. But his inclusion of the emperor among his heirs in his will was probably intended to secure decent treatment at least for his family. Instead it appears that the department of the financial procurator, Catus Decianus, behaved in a particularly high-handed fashion in claiming the kingdom for the emperor; the physical mishandling of Prasutagus' widow, Boudicca, and her daughters caused an outrage.

Although this was the dramatic cause of the rebellion that broke out in the province, other factors, too, appear to have played their part. It is possible that the magnitude of the task of conquering the whole of Britain was beginning to be appreciated. Indeed, there may even have been talk of withdrawal from Britain to cut Rome's losses. For whatever reason, some of those Romans who had invested money in Britain, significant among whom was Nero's tutor, Seneca, now sought to recall it. This clearly could not be done without inflicting financial hardship and, presumably, some physical hardship too in the exactions that followed.

All of this combined to precipitate what was probably the most serious provincial rebellion of the first century AD, when the Iceni and the Trinovantes made common cause in what is known as Boudicca's revolt (AD 60–61). The inception of the rebellion was made that much easier by the fact that the governor Paullinus was engaged in the far west and had the bulk of the province's four legions with him (II *Augusta*, IX *Hispana*, XIV *Gemina Martia Victrix*, XX *Valeria Victrix*).

According to Tacitus and Dio Cassius, the rebels meted out a terrible punishment to the Romanized towns of Verulamium (St Albans), Londinium (London) and particularly Camulodunum (Colchester), where the temple of the imperial cult was a principal objective. The temple was sacked, and the altar of Victoria outside it smashed; further, the statue of Claudius appears to have had its head wrenched from the body to be carried off as booty, and, to judge from its rediscovery in the river Alde in Suffolk, to have been given as an offering to a local deity to demonstrate the superiority of Celtic over Roman gods. Tacitus alleges that in this violent rampage some seventy thousand Romano-British were slaughtered, though he presumably exaggerates. The nearest legion (IX *Hispana*) was stopped in its tracks, and the rebellion was not checked until Paullinus abandoned his military operations in the west and returned to deal with the rebels himself.

It had been a traumatic episode, and it did not show Roman provincial administration in a favourable light. The offending procurator Decianus had fled, to be replaced by Julius Classicianus, who evidently reported to Nero on a range of problems in the province, including the governor's errors of judgement. As a result Nero sent Polyclitus, an ex-slave, to review the whole situation. This resulted in a change of policy; for the time being, further conquest was put on hold, and a new governor (Petronius Turpilianus) was sent out with a brief to conduct his government in such a way as to give wounds time to heal. So it remained until, in the course of the disturbances which followed Nero's death in AD 68, a new source of trouble emerged among the Brigantes of northern England.

If Britain provided the empire with one of its most serious rebellions, one of its longest-running difficulties was located in the east, and involved Rome's relations with the kingdom of Parthia. It focussed on the political orientation of the neighbouring kingdom of Armenia.

Asia Minor had long been an area of political complexity for Rome. After the wars in the first century BC against Mithridates, the king of Pontus, Pompey had created a political settlement which consisted of provinces around the coast of Asia Minor, and client–kingdoms ('Hellenistic monarchies') in the interior. Pro-Roman territory was thus brought to the border of Parthia, and in the last years of the republic at least two Roman armies came to grief in the area – those of Marcus Crassus in 53 BC., and Marcus Antonius' general, Decidius Saxa, in 36 BC. Augustus had made it one of his early priorities to restore Roman pride there and a pro-Roman equilibrium; the method employed was the installing on the throne of Armenia of a king who was acceptable both to Rome and Parthia; this had a chequered, but not totally unsatisfactory, history under the earlier Julio–Claudians.

In Claudius' later years, however, the area had fallen once again into political turmoil; in AD 47, on a request from the Parthians, Claudius sent Meherdates as their king; but in the absence of tangible Roman support, Meherdates soon fell, to be replaced by Vologaeses. Having installed one of his brothers as king of Media, in AD 52 Vologaeses tried to make the other, Tiridates, king of Armenia, when an opportunity was provided by the fall of its incumbent ruler, Mithridates. Tiridates was installed as a result of direct armed intervention in Armenia by the Parthians; for Rome this amounted to Armenia having become part of the Parthian empire, and it was not to be tolerated.

Throughout the Julio–Claudian period the chief Roman province in the east was Syria, whose governor was regarded as the empire's senior military personage. He had four legions under him (III *Gallica*, VI *Ferrata*, X *Fretensis* and XII *Fulminata*) which, despite the necessary qualification of Roman citizenship for legionary service, consisted almost entirely of local enlistments. No other provinces in Asia Minor had permanent legionary garrisons at this time.

Since this disturbed state of affairs greeted Nero on his accession, the new government was keen to make a dynamic impact. Within months, Gnaeus Domitius Corbulo was made governor of Cappadocia and Galatia with the principal responsibility of delivering Armenia from the Parthians. Three of Syria's legions (III, VI and X) were transferred to Cappadocia, and garrisons were adjusted elsewhere to keep the Syrian establishment up to strength (IV *Scythica*, V *Macedonica* and XV *Apollinaris*); there was no question of raising extra legions to cope with this crisis, and so risks had to be entertained in other areas.

Corbulo is noted by Tacitus chiefly for his stern and old-fashioned disciplinarianism, but it is evident that he was a diplomat, too. Instead of ousting Tiridates, he tried in AD 58 to persuade both him and Vologaeses to petition for Tiridates' formal recognition by Nero. Their unwillingness to do this forced Corbulo's hand and Tiridates was driven out, his place being taken by a pro-Roman nominee, Tigranes. By now, Corbulo had taken over Syria, requesting Nero to establish a separate command for Armenia. According to Tacitus, much that ensued amounted to diplomatic posturing, since (he says) Corbulo preferred not to have to make war, while Vologaeses, too, was anxious to avoid a military conflict with Rome. In the manoeuvring, Tigranes was removed and Vologaeses agreed to enter into negotiation for the recognition of Tiridates as king of Armenia.

The failure – for unknown reasons – of this negotiation led to a further switch of Roman policy. In AD 62 Caesennius Paetus was sent to Cappadocia, claiming that his brief was to reduce Armenia to the status of a province. Even so, Paetus does not appear to have been provocative; indeed, the blame for the resumption of hostilities lay with the Parthians. Yet even this would appear to have been largely accidental. Paetus lost heavily to Vologaeses at Rhandeia, despite the fact that a provocative defeat of Roman forces was still no part of Vologaeses' policy; in negotiations that followed he agreed to let Tiridates do homage to Rome in return for the Armenian throne – though not personally in Rome or in Nero's presence.

Again, a strong diplomatic card was played: Corbulo was given an overriding eastern command (*maius imperium*), as if the intention was now the complete reduction of Armenia to the status of a province. Under this pressure, Tiridates and Vologaeses agreed that the former would lay down his kingly diadem and would resume it only from Nero's hands in Rome.

Nero had secured peace across the world; the coinage duly reflected the fact by showing the temple of Janus in Rome, with its gates shut, symbolizing total world peace. The *princeps* also sought to extract the full measure of publicity from the outcome of events in the east. In an extremely impressive – and excessively costly – round of ceremonial, Tiridates came to Italy, accompanied by Parthian and Roman nobility (including Corbulo's son-in-law, Annius Vinicianus), to receive his diadem from Nero's hands: 'I have come to you, my God, worshipping you as Mithras.' This designation, which features in Dio's lengthy account of the occasion, well accords with forms of address, such as 'The New Apollo' and 'The New Sun', which were readily applied to Nero in the eastern part of the empire.

Dio also reports Tiridates' disgust at Nero's excessive behaviour, which is expressed in the form of surprise at Corbulo's continued willingness to serve such a master. But such observations on Dio's part are in tune with his desire to downgrade the significance of what had happened, and also perhaps to point a moral which would have been equally applicable in the historian's own day in the early third century AD.

How, then, should we assess the achievement? In the first

place, it should be noted that the final outcome was essentially what Corbulo had offered at the outset. In the meantime, Nero's government had displayed flexibility in its attempts to find a solution. Little face had been lost on the Roman side, with the exception of the defeat at Rhandeia which can be ascribed largely to Paetus' incompetence. Nero had shown strong loyalty to Corbulo and had facilitated his requests for reinforcements; for his part, while Corbulo had not been tested by having to fight a major battle, he had clearly been following an official line which looked, for a solution, to diplomacy backed by the power to convince the enemy that recourse to armed force would and could be had, if it were necessary – a reapplication of the formula successfully used by Augustus in the twenties BC. In this sense, despite Tacitus' apparent misgivings over Corbulo's arrogance and lack of co-operativeness, the general had adhered firmly to his emperor's policy which ultimately had achieved the desired result. It is also likely that, despite Dio's misgivings, in the final acts of diplomacy in AD 66, Nero had by his behaviour 'talked a language' which was well understood by Tiridates and Vologaeses; otherwise they would have accepted this solution at an earlier stage in the proceedings.

It was also a valuable achievement to have ascertained the Parthian unwillingness to fight on a large scale. Further, the solution lasted and provided peace in the area; the importance of this can be measured by the Roman ability between AD 67 and 70 to divert large numbers of the Syrian legions to the problems of Judaea, by their ability to conduct several other smaller rearrangements of client–kingdoms in the area, and to turn their attention, without apparent risk to stability, to the events of the civil war in which eastern commanders and troops were heavily involved in AD 69–70. Further, Vespasian was able to undertake with impunity far-reaching reorganization in Asia Minor in the early seventies. Nero's peace should thus not be lightly dismissed. Despite a lack of personal military experience and inclination, he had been prepared to trust and back those who had. He had also been sufficiently flexible in attitude to adjust policy when advised to do this. It might even be argued that the excessive attention which he paid to the east in his later years was at least in part aimed at raising morale in the area and thus buttressing the eastern provinces against future military and political adventurism on the part of the Parthians. As we have seen, the events of the immediate future put Nero's arrangements to the test, and they measured up to that test.

As has been noted, an immediate dividend of the peace was Rome's ability in the last years of Nero's reign to turn its full attention to the mounting problems of Judaea, which broke into open warfare in AD 67. The problems which came to a head in Nero's reign were not new, and in no way offer a specific comment on the quality of provincial government at that period.

Essentially the Jewish state and domination by Rome were incompatible ideas, since many Jews looked not just towards independence from Rome but to domination of the world *by themselves*. Judaea had been a province under an equestrian procurator since Augustus' time, with the exception of a brief return to a client–monarchy under Claudius' friend, Herod Agrippa, between AD 41 and 44. The procurators tended to work through the Sadducees, though the feuding within this group made them rather ineffective. On the other hand, the Pharisees were more alive to the desired destiny of a Jewish state, particularly the most extreme of their group, the Zealots.

There is little indication that the standard of provincial government in Judaea had been particularly low, although Caligula's decision to have his statue erected in the Temple at Jerusalem had caused a furore until it was rescinded. Tacitus alleges that Antonius Felix (procurator, AD 52–60) had behaved high-handedly, though this may reflect no more than the historian's antipathy towards a man whose brother was Claudius' freedman, Pallas. The immediate cause of the trouble in Nero's reign appears to have been the decision in AD 66 of the procurator, Gessius Florus, to infringe the Temple sanctuary by taking from the treasury money which was 'due to Caesar'.

Riots broke out in Jerusalem, and a fortress at Masada was taken and its garrison annihilated; simultaneous disturbances broke out among Jews of the *Diaspora*, and in Egypt, the prefect Tiberius Julius Alexander used legionary troops to quell riots in Alexandria. If war was not already inevitable, it was made so when Cestius Gallus (governor of Syria), who had entered Judaea with legionary troops, was attacked. The death of Gallus during the winter of AD 66–67 enabled Nero to introduce revised arrangements in the area.

Licinius Mucianus was sent out as the new governor of Syria, and a new Judaean command established under the future emperor, Vespasian. Whatever the qualities of these men, it has been pointed out that their humble origins appear to indicate a new policy on Nero's part, probably born of the conspiracies of AD 65 and 66 (see below), of appointing to senior commands men whose origins made them unlikely rivals to Nero's own position. This policy, seen also in the case of Verginius Rufus in Upper Germany, marked a sharp departure from the strength that had characterized Nero's earlier appointments.

Vespasian was given three legions – V *Macedonica* and X *Fretensis* (from Syria) and XV *Apollinaris* (formerly a Danubian legion, which had been transferred to Syria, and thence to Egypt); with them he worked systematically through Judaea, and was in position to besiege Jerusalem by the summer of AD 68, when news came of Nero's death. This led to an interruption of operations, while Vespasian and Mucianus consulted on political matters leading to a decision in AD 69 by Vespasian to put himself forward as a candidate for imperial power.

Jerusalem eventually fell to Vespasian's son, Titus, in the summer of AD 70, though resistance continued in Judaea until the fall of Masada in AD 73. The Temple was destroyed in an effort to break the heart of Jewish nationhood; although the payments which all Jews traditionally made to the Temple were transferred to Jupiter Capitolinus in Rome, the basic privileges which the Romans had long accorded to the Jews remained: local freedom of worship, together with immunity from military service and from imperial cult worship. The Roman victory was celebrated in Rome, and scenes from the celebrations can be seen on the Arch of Titus, which was erected at the southern end of the *via sacra*, the road leading out of the Forum.

Thus in the major fields of imperial conflict during his reign, Nero can be seen to have acted sensibly, choosing sound commanders, trusting them to do their jobs and providing them with the necessary resources. What perhaps is more questionable, in some instances at least, is the standard of provincial government which in some cases precipitated the crises.

Nero succeeded an emperor who had been concerned about the integration of the empire and the steps necessary to achieve it. *Colonia* foundation and franchise grants were not, however, pursued uncritically. Rome and Italy, and the defence of them, remained the cornerstones of Claudius' policy; there was no question of downgrading Italy, as effectively happened later, in favour of provincial advancement. In particular, citizenship was extended to 'deserving cases', and those who did not show sufficient commitment were not so privileged. As a consequence, most of Claudius' grants were in the west, although to some extent the progress of applications for advancement was disfigured by corruption. Claudius evidently believed that talent, whatever its origin, should be harnessed, and that those with a contribution to make should be empowered to make it. He also held that restrictiveness over privileges was ultimately self-defeating, and no doubt recognized that a willing empire would be more economical to govern, with greater benefits accruing to the centre.

Nero was far less open-handed in grants of citizenship and in town foundation; even his much-proclaimed Hellenism did not lead to major advances of this nature in the east, except perhaps in Greece itself, and even then largely in the context of his visit to Greece in AD 67. In any case, the commonest route to citizenship – that is, through military service – hardly applied to Greeks.

Advances in the Romanization of the west continued, and wealthy aristocrats from areas such as Spain and Gaul could make an impact locally and perhaps subsequently on a wider stage. But Romanization needed to develop further before major advances for large numbers of people could be contemplated; many people were reluctant to shed their older ways, and so in the west tribal loyalties were still important (as is shown by the Gallo-German uprising of AD 69–70), while for easterners city life remained a magnetic force. As we have seen, Nero's government proposed, though did not pursue, a way of enhancing the wealth of provincials by waiving indirect taxation: this would at one and the same time have freed up trade, and allowed those involved to become wealthier. Insufficient wealth, after all, posed the greatest obstacle confronting those who wished to advance themselves. Although the proposal fell, measures were taken to curb the exactions in the provinces of the emperor's financial agents (procurators). In essence Romanization still needed to progress at a lower level in most areas; thus, enhancing the level of recruitment into auxiliary units of the Roman army was a smaller, but at this stage a more practical, step for most.

Nonetheless the prosperity of the provinces clearly developed during the period, and in some senses the tangible results of this can be seen in the years following Nero's reign; for example, in the seventies, of those senators whose origins are known 83.2 per cent were Italian and 16.8 per cent provincial; by the early second century, 65.8 per cent were of Italian origin and 34.2 per cent provincial. Of those provincial senators, in Vespasian's reign 70 per cent were from western European provinces and 30 per cent from elsewhere; by Trajan's time, those with a western European origin had fallen to 55.8 per cent. Such figures, while based inevitably on incomplete information, nevertheless provide a general indication of trends.

The Jewish historian Josephus refers to Gaul as 'flooding almost the entire world with its products'; Africa in AD 68 was sufficiently prosperous to allow Lucius Clodius Macer to pose a real risk to Italy by threatening to discontinue grain supplies from the province. By the second and third centuries AD Africa had become one of the most prosperous areas of the empire, as the quality of its surviving buildings amply demonstrates.

Alongside a real, if undramatic, enhancement in prosperity, we should note – at least as far as Tacitean examples allow us – a readiness on the government's part to come down hard on officials guilty of extortion: where cases were proven, punishments could be severe, as in the case of Cossutianus Capito (in Cilicia in AD 57) who was expelled from the senate (though later reinstated through the influence of his father-in-law, Tigellinus). It remained, however, relatively expensive for a province to bring a prosecution, particularly since on Juvenal's evidence it was quite likely that a successful prosecution would not be followed by financial restitution. Nero also dealt with other forms of official corruption, such as the taking of bribes for favours and the publication of lavish shows which, Tacitus says, were often as oppressive to provincials as actual extortion. Also attacked was the practice on the part of some governors of covering themselves with 'favourable references' from corrupt and oppressive local grandees.

Most of the evidence for Nero's reign comes from the earlier years, but the continued absence of clear signs of provincial discontent in the later years makes it likely that the lack of documentary evidence is due more to changing preoccupations on the part of the historians than to dramatic changes in the quality of provincial government. It can be assumed that in general the far higher standard of provincial government that characterized the Augustan principate was maintained by this last descendant of Augustus.

4

Hellenistic monarch or Roman megalomaniac?

That Nero became increasingly self-centred, arbitrary and capricious in his government is in little doubt; but did he consciously embrace a philosophy of ruling to which the closest parallels would have been found among the Hellenistic monarchs of Asia Minor? Although he was certainly a devotee of Greek culture, did he wish to live as a Greek, even to the point of moving the empire's centre from Rome to Alexandria?

Since the conquest of Greece by Rome in the second century BC the Roman governing class had reacted to Greek culture in a variety of ways. In the arts, Greek influence had been pervasive: Roman literature had adopted many Greek forms, and existing forms had been changed by Greek influences. Nothing shows this better than the contrast between the neo-Hellenistic poetry of Catullus in the first century BC and the archaic epic style of his contemporary, Lucretius, although the latter was using his traditional style as a vehicle to communicate the atomic theory of the Greek Democritus. At the same time, Cicero was producing a Latin vocabulary for the translation and imitation of the Greek philosophers, and demonstrated the duality of his culture by producing histories of his consulship in Latin and Greek – both in prose and in verse. Virgil's great national epic, the *Aeneid*, was heralded by his contemporary Propertius with the exclamation that 'something greater than the *Iliad* has been born'. The Augustan poet Horace well caught the atmosphere

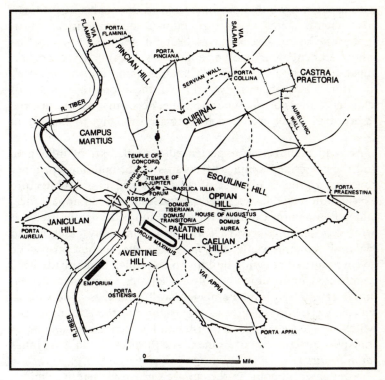

3. Neronian Rome

when he wrote that 'captive Greece has taken captive her savage captor, and introduced the arts to rustic Latium'. Elsewhere he enjoined the Roman writer to study his Greek originals night and day.

The Greek influence pervaded other areas of art and thought: Scipio Aemilianus utilized the services of the historian Polybius who brought a whole new dimension to the analysis of Roman government, which in its turn influenced the political philosophy of Cicero. Greek slaves brought new subjects into the school student's curriculum, and Greek became a second language for Rome's aristocracy. Claudius' familiarity with Greek literature was sufficiently well known for a joke to be made of it in Seneca's *Apocolocyntosis*, while, according to Tacitus, the reserved Tiberius muttered his private thoughts to himself in Greek.

Art and architecture experienced a similar set of influences and the essentially simple, Etruscan style of building in timber gave way to the regular use of the Greek orders of architecture executed in stone. Greek building styles made their appearance, and in Pompeii for example we see the simple Italian house built around a single courtyard transformed in many cases into a 'palatial' structure centred upon two (or more) courtyards. The lavish nature of personal building plans which had already been commented upon unfavourably by Horace went on unabated into Nero's reign, and Pompeian wall paintings – as well as surviving structures – give us an insight into the level of luxury which was accepted as a norm, and which Nero sought to transport into the city of Rome in the form of his Golden House (*domus aurea*).

From an early point in the empire's growth, eastern religious practices had begun to make an impact on Rome; a senatorial decree of 186 BC on Dionysiac worship indicates the alarm with which this was viewed – and not surprisingly, for such practices were seen as threatening the moral fibre of the republic, and offering to individuals focal points of religious loyalty outside the corporate religion of the state. However, the development of such practices in the city did not stop, and the government generally contented itself with tolerating all but outrageous, disruptive or subversive practices; thus, Tiberius in AD 19 moved to outlaw Egyptian and Jewish religious activities in Rome, while Caligula planned (though later withdrew) a harsh imposition on the Jews for their destruction of an imperial cult altar built by Greeks at Jamnia.

The imperial cult represented a development of what was an essentially eastern practice, which during the late republican period manifested itself in the worship in former Hellenistic kingdoms of 'Rome and the senate'. Such a focussing of attention on to the ruler was seen by Augustus as a useful adjunct to his powers, and he harnessed the cult of *Rome and Augustus* to the Roman state religion. He did not see himself as a god, but rather as the inspired and appointed guardian of Rome. Indeed, he and Tiberius set their faces firmly against extravagant development of the practice, realizing that their status as *principes* ('leading citizens') counselled caution in a field that was sensitive in the west; any suggestion that they were 'kings', let alone 'gods', could have spelled political disaster. It was this balance of caution and the desire to exploit popular enthusiasm that led to the inception of the cult of *Rome and Augustus*.

More than once Tiberius made known to provincials who wished to worship him his temperamental distaste for such extravagance; his reply to the people of Gytheum (in Sparta) was typical:

Tiberius Caesar Augustus, son of Augustus, *pontifex maximus*, holding the tribunician power for the [sixteenth] year, to the superintendents and city of Gytheum, greeting. Decimus Turranius Nicanor, the envoy sent by you to me and my mother, gave me your letter to which were appended the measures passed by you in veneration of my father and in our honour. I recommend you for this and consider that it is fitting for all men in general and for your city in particular to reserve special honours befitting the gods in keeping with the greatness of the services of my father to the whole world; but I myself am satisfied with more moderate honours suitable for men. My mother, however, will reply to you when she hears your decision about honours for her.

This response is closely mirrored by Tacitus' account of a reply in a similar vein to a request that came from Spain (*Annals* IV. 37–8):

At about this same time the people of Further Spain sent ambassadors to seek permission to follow in Asia's footsteps

43

and build a shrine to Tiberius and his mother. Tiberius was generally firm in refusing such honours, but thought that he should take the opportunity to silence rumours that he was becoming less scrupulous in this matter. So he made a speech in the following terms: 'Senators, I am fully aware that there have been those who have noted inconsistency in my behaviour when I recently failed to oppose a similar request to this, that was being made by the communities of Asia. I shall thus use this occasion to explain why I allowed the people of Asia their request, and what my future policy in this field is to be. I treat as law everything that was done or said by the Divine Augustus. He did not refuse the people of Pergamum permission to build a temple to himself and to the city of Rome. With his example behind me I more readily agreed to Asia's request because the people there proposed to conjoin my cult with worship of the senate. However, whilst to have granted one such request may be pardonable, it would be arrogant and over-bearing to have my statue worshipped along with those of the Gods in every province. In any case, the honour implied in the Augustan example will pale if it becomes part of the commonplace of flattery.'

'Senators, I am a human being, performing human tasks, and it is my ambition to fulfil the role of *princeps*. I want you to understand this, and I want future generations to believe it; you and they will do more than adequate service to my reputation if I am held to be worthy of my forebears, careful for your interests, steadfast in danger, and not afraid to be unpopular if I am serving the national good. As far as I am concerned, if you hold these opinions of me, they will stand as my temples and my finest statues, and they will last. For if posterity's judgement turns adversely, then stone structures are regarded as if they were the tombstones of people who do not deserve respect. So my prayer to the Gods is that so long as I live they should grant me an easy conscience and a mind that knows its duty to Gods and men. To provincials and Roman citizens, I pray that when I am dead my actions and reputation should be praised and well remembered.' After this, in private conversation, too, he persisted in his objections to such a personalised cult. Some regarded this as a sign of genuine modesty, whilst others attributed it to uneasiness on his part.

44

Despite the fact that there was generally a greater degree of imperial tolerance with regard to the Hellenistic east, where such practices were normal, Germanicus, the adopted son of Tiberius, showed a distaste for divine honours offered him by Egyptians:

> Germanicus Caesar, son of Augustus, grandson of the deified Augustus, proconsul, says:
> 'Your good-will, which you display whenever you see me, I welcome, but your acclamations, which are odious to me and which are suited to the gods, I wholly reject. For they are suitable only for the one who is indeed the saviour and the benefactor of the whole human race, my father, and to his mother, my grandmother. My position is consequent upon their divinity, so that, if you disobey me, you will compel me to appear before you less frequently.'

Caligula evidently pursued a more relaxed policy in the east, though suggestions in the written sources that he tried to extend worship of himself into Italy, and thought of himself as a living deity are not supported by unequivocal material evidence. Clearly the practice of deifying certain dead emperors had implications: the successor may have felt boosted by the title, 'son of God', and Caligula, according to Philo, seems to have considered himself thus enhanced by his descent from Augustus; his completion of the temple, begun by Tiberius, to *Divus Augustus* will not have been a mere accident. Whatever view was taken by the senatorial aristocracy of Claudius' deification, Nero's standing will clearly have been enhanced by it.

Obviously Hellenizing (or even Orientalizing) was not universally welcome; in its early days, traditionalists had vainly attempted to hold back the tide, and the 'classical' style of Augustan architecture was an attempt at a compromise. In literature, Lucan's annoyance at Nero's rivalry was the epic poet's alleged motive for joining the Pisonian conspiracy of AD 65 (see below in Chapter 5). Juvenal attacked Rome as a 'Greek city' and poured contempt on what he called the 'oriental sewerage', which he alleged was filling Rome at the turn of the first and second centuries AD.

Thus, we need to see how far Nero fits into the context of such cultural and political Hellenizing. As we have seen, it was Seneca's aim to present Nero with what he regarded as a clear statement of the Augustan model for government; this, however, included an emphasis on virtues, such as clemency (*clementia*), which were supposedly concerned with moderation in relationships between ruler and ruled. Such a virtue was in reality distant from Roman tradition, in that clemency could be taken away as easily as it was bestowed, and was thus, as Cassius had observed of Caesar, a mark of *dominatio* rather than of equality of status. Thus the Augustan model, as it was advanced by Seneca, was potentially a blueprint for arbitrary government, even though such virtues might be popular and welcome – so long as they lasted. Tiberius' principate had graphically illustrated the danger of reliance upon imperial clemency and goodwill.

It has been noted that such was the senate's attitude to Nero from the earliest days of his principate that he was inevitably elevated as if on to a pedestal. The logic was that if Nero saw good deeds made him popular, then he would be persuaded to do more. He clearly relished favourable reactions to his spontaneous good deeds, but was angry by the same measure if his generosity seemed to have been rejected – as was shown by his dismissal of Pallas following Agrippina's churlish attitude to a gift from Nero. A similar point is made by Tacitus in his observation that Nero hoped to calm disquiet at the murder of Britannicus by acts of generosity. At the same time he requested the support of the senate and people, and the senate's extravagant reaction to Corbulo's successes in the east in AD 58 was to hail the *princeps* as victor, and to vote him statues, arches and consulships. In short, Nero liked to be extravagantly generous and he liked his generosity to be reciprocated with equally extravagant expressions of gratitude.

Similarly, he liked to pursue his own interests without check or criticism; the course of his affair with Acte and his carousing in the streets of Rome, which grew increasingly disorderly and vicious, demonstrate this. Nero, in short, can be characterized as a young man who liked to do as he pleased, and who, as he became more confident of his position, realized that there was little anyone could do to stop him.

Such irresponsibility soon bridged the gap between private and public matters; his treatment of those of whom he was fearful or envious grew harsher, more capricious and more open – as is demonstrated, in one version of the story, by the effective banishment of his former friend, the future emperor Marcus Salvius Otho, because of their shared obsession with Otho's wife, Poppaea Sabina. He required a senator, Julius Montanus, who had unknowingly hit him in one of his nocturnal 'events', to commit suicide, while Faustus Sulla was exiled because Nero thought (wrongly) that Sulla had tried to ambush him in similar circumstances.

The climax of such an 'emancipation' was reached with the murder of his mother. Despite his fears, Nero came through this traumatic act with his popularity apparently undiminished – a reflection perhaps of the deteriorating quality of the people with whom by that time he was coming to surround himself. Tacitus' later description is striking:

> Nero lingered in the cities of Campania. His return to Rome was a worrying problem. Would the senate be obedient? Would the public cheer him? Every bad character (and no court had ever had so many) reassured him that Agrippina was detested, and that her death had increased his popularity. They urged him to enter boldly and see for himself how he was revered. Preceding him – as they had asked to – they found even greater enthusiasm than they had promised. The people marshalled in their tribes were out to meet him, the senators were in their fine clothes, wives and children drawn up in lines by sex and age. Along his route there were tiers of seats as though for a triumph. Proud conqueror of a servile nation, Nero proceeded to the Capitol and paid his vows. Then he plunged into the wildest improprieties, which vestiges of respect for his mother had hitherto not indeed repressed, but impeded.

The character of such behaviour owes nothing to Hellenizing; it represents the progressive effect of over-pampered self-indulgence.

As Tacitus suggests, the impetus towards overt Hellenizing came with his mother's death; its appearance then does not represent a cultural change in Nero, but rather a freedom to do in public what his advisers had tried till then to restrict to the emperor's private moments. Although the emperor had not completed a traditional education with a spell in a rhetorical school in Greece, he had, according to Tacitus, from a very early stage in his life shown an interest in cultural matters, including the writing of poetry, singing and painting; nor is the historian uncomplimentary about Nero's early success in these fields. Perhaps the later manifestation of what has been interpreted as Nero's Hellenism had its origins in little more than the cultural interests common to many young Romans and a sense of the theatrical which Nero possibly inherited from his grandfather, Germanicus, and shared with Germanicus' youngest son, Gaius Caligula.

The strength of Nero's desire to make these interests public after his mother's death is probably explained by the degree of resentment he felt since he had needed to keep them hidden while she was alive. The context, therefore, in which they became public inevitably made them an issue of political significance. If Tacitus is to be believed, this happened very shortly after Agrippina's murder. Seneca and Burrus managed to confine Nero's charioteering to a largely private venue, but the Youth Games (*Juvenalia*) were more public, involving men and women of the upper classes of Roman society in theatrical performances in Latin and Greek. The involvement of members of the senatorial and equestrian orders, while illegal in Rome, indicates the Greek notion that competitive performances in public were a mark of their heroic ideal. The formation of a group of young equestrians (*Augustiani*), who were to form Nero's bodyguard and cheerleaders on such occasions, represents a further Hellenistic importation into Rome.

The following year, in AD 60, the quinquennial *Neroneia* were introduced – competitions in poetry, music, athletics and racing; while these involved largely Greek protagonists in the first instance, Nero soon tried to encourage Rome's upper classes to take part. Indeed, in the second celebration – in AD 65 – he participated himself, supposedly, according to Suetonius, by popular request. His models were Homeric contests and the great festivals celebrated by the Greek poet, Pindar. It may be significant that his own *first* public performance had taken place the previous year in that most Greek of Italian cities, Neapolis (Naples). While Hellenizing was involved in this, and while it not surprisingly incurred the displeasure of traditionalists, we need not assume, as some evidently did, that Nero's purpose was to degrade the upper classes. On the contrary, he probably believed that Greek contests in a variety of skills were more civilized than the more earthy Roman festivals, the traditions of which were firmly embedded in ancient life-and-death rituals. To many these must have appeared sordid displays, particularly when, as had happened in Pompeii in AD 59, a gladiatorial contest had precipitated crowd violence – a scene depicted on a wall painting in Pompeii – leading to the closure of the town's amphitheatre for a period of ten years.

Hellenizing did not, however, stop with public performance. The pillaging of Greek works of art recalled earlier days of Roman imperialism. This may, along with the increasing Hellenizing of architectural and interior design, have pointed towards an increasing desire on Nero's part to isolate himself from unreceptive Roman tastes, and concentrate his interests upon those parts of the empire which seemed more in tune with his tastes – the Greek cities of Italy and mainland Greece. This culminated in AD 66–67 with his visit to Greece, along with senators, praetorians and his *Augustiani*.

Nero participated in all of the great festivals (Olympian, Delphic, Isthmian and Nemean), winning (inevitably) 1,808 first prizes. The grandness of his vision, however, encompassed projects other than the artistic, although these were clearly of great significance to him. He began to construct a canal through the isthmus at Corinth, imitating the Hellenistic king Demetrius and his own ancestors Julius Caesar and Gaius Caligula. The project was launched with enthusiasm and determination, involving (among others) six thousand captives from the Jewish war, but was never finished.

The most grandiose conception, however, of Nero's visit was his new 'Liberation of Hellas', in imitation of the famous declaration of 196 BC by Flamininus following the defeat of the Macedonian king, Philip V. The text of Nero's declaration survives (preserved at Acraephia in Boeotia): 'The emperor Caesar says: "Wishing to thank most noble Hellas for its goodwill and reverence towards me, I order as many inhabitants of the provinces as possible to come to Corinth on 28 November."'

When the crowds had gathered in the place of assembly he spoke the following words:

Men of Hellas, I give you an unlooked-for gift – if indeed anything may not be hoped for from one of my greatness of mind – a gift so great, you were incapable of asking for it. All Greeks inhabiting Achaea and the land called till now the

Peloponnese receive freedom and immunity from taxes, something which not all of you enjoyed even in your happiest days; for you were subject to strangers or to each other. I wish I were giving this gift when Hellas was still flourishing so that more people might enjoy the benefit, and I blame time itself for spending in advance the greatness of my gifts. But I am bestowing this benefaction on you not out of pity but out of goodwill, in recompense to your gods whose care for me both on land and on sea I have never found wanting, and who are affording me an opportunity to bestow so great a benefaction; for other rulers have granted freedom to cities, but Nero alone to an entire province.

It is difficult to estimate the real value of the gesture, since it was soon cancelled by the emperor Vespasian (AD 69–79). Greek writers, however, into the second century AD afforded it a prominence which indicates that psychologically at least it meant a great deal to Greeks – as undoubtedly Nero, in a display of generosity that was typical of him, intended it to. The emperor's popularity in the eastern half of his empire can perhaps in part be measured by the appearance in AD 88 of a 'false Nero'.

Nero's generosity was amply repaid, not just by his popularity in the region, but by the frequent divine acclamations of him – Nero Zeus the Liberator, Nero–Apollo, Nero–Helios, the New Sun, the Saviour and Benefactor of the whole world, among others. The third-century historian Dio Cassius indicates that Nero received these and other acclamations when he returned to Italy after the visit to Greece.

Clearly such acclamations prompt us to ask questions concerning Nero's view of his status, as man or god, particularly since it would not be difficult to find indications of megalomania in what the *princeps* both said and did. As we have seen, to Romans, worship of the ruler as a living god was not a natural phenomenon: indeed, such elevation went far beyond the aristocratic corporateness which was a traditional feature of Roman political life, and which, ostensibly at least, Augustus had tried to strengthen. However his achievement in bringing order out of chaos had seemed to many to have been almost superhuman, and in any case, the posthumous deification of Julius Caesar had made Augustus 'son of god' (*divi filius*). Further, Augustus stressed his 'divine connections' by emphasizing the Julian family's descent from Venus and the special protection which he claimed from Apollo. Augustan architectural monuments such as the *Altar of Augustan Peace* make these connections specifically. Further, the contemporary 'court-poet' Horace wrote that Augustus would be considered 'a god on earth' (*praesens divus*) – equivalent to Jupiter in heaven – if he were to add Britain and Parthia to the Roman empire. However, as Tiberius' responses showed (see above on pp. 43f), there was a world of difference between what was offered by enthusiastic subjects and what may have been required, or even demanded, by the *princeps* himself. For Romans the dividing line between divine acclamations and sheer extravagant theatricality might on occasion be a narrow one: both Germanicus and his son Caligula received extravagant compliments in the east and, to some extent, encouraged these by likening themselves to Alexander the Great. However, that either of these men, both of whom were closely related to Nero, saw themselves as gods on earth is a contention unsupported by surviving material evidence – despite allegations in the sources to that effect in the case of Caligula.

That Nero's proclamations showed signs of megalomania is hardly in doubt, but was he trying to establish himself as a god on earth? No cult paraphernalia survives in the west, although the coinage of Nero's later years bears examination in this connection; indeed, it might be argued that Nero's behaviour in his last *quinquennium*, backed by such incidents as Tiridates' hailing of him as *Mithras* in AD 66, does offer a coherent pattern of an increasing preoccupation on Nero's part with his own status.

It certainly cannot be said that Nero's later coinage offers unequivocal evidence of divine pretensions; indeed, the issue of coins bearing such an interpretation was mixed in with issues of a far more traditional type, commemorating notable events, as when in AD 66 the eastern war came to a satisfactory conclusion. Nor should we perhaps worry too much about the issue of *dupondii*, showing Nero's head on the obverse side wearing the radiate crown of the sun. It is impossible now to be certain what Nero intended to convey by this, for Nero was the first emperor to issue all *aes* denominations in both copper and the alloy, orichalcum: previously denominations could be distinguished by the different appearance of the metal employed for each of them, but the similar sizes of *dupondii* and *asses* left them open to confusion when both appeared in both metals. In these circumstances, the use of the radiate crown on the *dupondius* might be no more sinister than providing a means to distinguish two denominations of otherwise similar appearance. Certainly most of Nero's successors used it for just this purpose – though ironically Hadrian, the most Hellenophile of later emperors, partly abandoned the convention. It has, however, to be said that previous to Nero's reign, the use of the radiate crown on the coinage was associated with the deified Augustus – that is, after his death and deification in AD 14.

There is no doubt that many of Nero's later coin types are capable of being interpreted as bearing a more specific connection between the emperor and divinity. Particularly arresting is his issue of AD 65 depicting Apollo–Citharoedus ('the lyre-player') on the reverse. The coin was sufficiently striking to be one of the few ever to be mentioned by an ancient author (Suetonius, *Life of Nero* 25). It is less clear, of course, whether Nero intended to portray himself as Nero–Apollo or simply to advertise the god who was the patron of his musical performances; perhaps the doubt was deliberately created, so that the coin could be looked at in different ways according to taste and conviction. However, Nero's own conviction on the matter may be judged from the establishment of a cult of 'the Heavenly Voice', and from the fact that Nero is recorded as having dressed as Apollo–Citharoedus. Significant too perhaps is the adoption of Apollo-like features in Nero's obverse portrait, particularly the depiction of the growth of hair down the back of his neck.

The commemoration on the coinage, following the detection of the Pisonian conspiracy in AD 65, of *Jupiter Custos* ('the Guardian') and *Salus* ('Health and Safety') might not be seen as any more significant than an honouring of relevant gods and personified virtues; however, the Apollo coin casts doubts even over these issues. Also striking are *denarii* on which Nero and Poppaea Sabina are depicted radiate on the reverses. It is true that *Sol* ('the Sun') was credited with the unmasking of the Pisonian conspiracy, but such representations suggest more than this, and recall the use of the device in deification – different from its appearance on the obverse – the acclamations as the 'New Sun' which Nero received in the east, Tiridates' salutation of him as Mithras, and the appearance of the 'Sun-King' on the Colossus which stood at the entrance of Nero's new 'palace', the *domus aurea*. At the very least it can be said that such representations went well beyond what had been done by any of Nero's Julio–Claudian predecessors, and are evidence of his developing megalomania – if not more.

Nero's arbitrariness and megalomania provide the real keys to his growing unpopularity – at least in senatorial circles – in his last years. Crucial in this development was the great fire of AD 64 and its sequel and consequences. This event has been brought alive to most modern students by the allegation, made by Suetonius and Dio Cassius, that the emperor watched the conflagration, singing his poem on *The Sack of Troy*. With its heavy use of timber construction and the crowding of its buildings, Rome was subject to frequent serious fires. Even by Rome's standards, however, the fire of AD 64 was devastating. Large areas were seriously damaged or totally destroyed, including Nero's existing palace on the Palatine Hill, the *domus transitoria*, of which small portions can now be seen beneath the ruins of Domitian's palace, the *domus Augustana*. A considerable number of mansions and antique temples were also lost.

From the start, there were doubts as to whether the fire was accidental or was started by Nero himself, either for poetic inspiration or to provide the opportunity for substantial rebuilding. Tacitus, though mentioning the charge of arson, placed no credence in it. Indeed Nero, who was not in the city when the fire started, was on his return vigorous in the measures he took to relieve loss and suffering. In reality, we need no explanation beyond Rome's susceptibility to fire and the fact that a strong wind was blowing at the time of the outbreak, which went on for a week before a policy of deliberate demolition in its path starved it.

The fire is, of course, famous for what Tacitus treats as its sequel – the attack on Christians who suffered a variety of punishments, burning alive, crucifixion and being eaten alive by beasts. Of these punishments, death by fire was the regular punishment for arsonists, while the other two were normal for people of non-citizen or servile origin. Although Tacitus connects the attack on the Christians with Nero's need for a scapegoat to allay suspicion that he had caused the fire, other sources keep the events separate: Eusebius in the fourth century, for example, dated the martyrdom of Peter and Paul to the last year of Nero's reign. Whatever the truth of this, Nero's attack did not represent persecution of Christians for their faith, but rather the punishment of criminals for a range of assumed misdeeds, perhaps as an expiatory offering to the gods whose anger was supposedly symbolized by the fire.

Suspicions about Nero were not allayed; indeed, they were intensified by the scale of the building which he set in train. Tacitus, however, indicates that Nero was far-sighted and generous in his handling of the consequences of the disaster, and endeavoured to ensure by new building regulations that it should not occur again. The historian plainly saw Nero's Rome as a marked improvement upon its predecessor – both from the aesthetic point of view and because of its enhanced safety. He further suggests that Nero's building enthusiasms were fanned by Severus and Celer, a pair of engineers with extravagant ideas. Despite the constructive aspects of Nero's rebuilding plans, two projects in particular were taken to characterize the megalomania of the emperor and his planners – the scheme to cut a canal from Lake Avernus to the Tiber estuary (which was ultimately frustrated), and the design and construction of an extensive new palace, the *domus aurea*, which involved the landscaping of large parts of the Palatine, Esquiline and Caelian Hills.

It is clear that the large-scale landscaping and engineering wonders involved in the palace excited great criticism: both Tacitus and Suetonius give striking descriptions of revolving rooms, perfumed sprays, decoration with gold and jewels, together with 'lawns, lakes and faked rusticity' (see Appendix II). The project can be viewed in a number of ways: that it was exceedingly expensive can hardly be doubted, nor that it occupied an inordinate amount of space, which became even in antiquity the subject of cynical humour alleging that 'the whole of Rome is being turned into a villa'. Nor can many have found it easy to resist the conviction that Nero had 'profited by his country's ruin'.

The space involved and the nature of the construction itself were open to serious objection, for it devoured valuable urban space with buildings which were better suited to a rural setting. Indeed, it is tempting to speculate that it would have aroused little comment if it had been placed in a 'suitable environment'; wall paintings at sites in the Bay of Naples suggest that such villas were not unknown there, and one even illustrates the type of polygonal sun-court that was a central feature of the *domus aurea*. For many, therefore, the scheme as conceived will have confirmed their impression of the emperor's megalomania.

However, from the point of view of the development of Roman architecture, the *domus aurea* is a significant building – and not just because of its scale and engineering wonders. In its polygonal sun court and its octagonal dining room with its concrete-domed roof, it displays imagination and confidence in its use of materials. It has been said of the *domus aurea* that it 'ended the tyranny of the right angle' in Roman architecture.

Yet its partial remains provide a sinister comment on the *princeps*. It consists of a warren of corridors, many of them subterranean, and it was provided with 'false vistas' of the outdoor world through its wall decorations. The building and the *cryptoporticus*, which linked it to the Palatine Hill, suggest an emperor shunning his public and avoiding the daylight, alone in his megalomaniac world.

Given the reputation of its owner and the nature of the building itself, it is hardly surprising that, left unfinished at Nero's death, it held little attraction for his successors. Otho is said to have used it, while Vitellius disliked it. Its 'epitaph' was the Colosseum which Vespasian constructed on the spot where the Colossus, the column bearing the statue of Nero–Apollo, had stood (and whose enormous base has recently been revealed by excavation), and the tons of rubble which Trajan poured into its empty corridors to strengthen them sufficiently to bear the weight of the baths which he built on top of Nero's palace.

How then are we to assess the dilemma expressed in the title of the present chapter? It is evident that despite Agrippina's attempts to check Nero's youthful enthusiasms in the field of Greek culture, and rein it back to something more in keeping with tradition, Nero retained his level of enthusiasm throughout his life. That the *princeps* was a practitioner of some accomplishment in Hellenistic poetry seems to be in little doubt, though it is equally clear that he became excessively conceited regarding this: his reported dying words (*qualis opifex pereo*, or 'what an artist dies in me') appear to confirm this.

Equally clearly his enthusiasm for Greek culture spilled over into less desirable outlets which, because he was emperor of Rome, were likely to attract adverse comment. The introduction of his preferred styles of entertainment into the public domain, and his attempt to make his contemporaries share them, were ill-judged in the extreme. It tells us perhaps that besides being an enthusiast for Greek culture Nero also suffered from an immaturity of judgement, and failed to appreciate that there were private predilections which had no place in the public arena. The example of a later successor, Severus Alexander (AD 222–235), adequately illustrates the point by the contrast which it affords with Nero's behaviour. Although a devotee of sun worship and Mithraism, Severus Alexander did not allow these essentially private interests to obtrude on to the performance of his public duties. It may well also have been a symptom of Nero's growing megalomania that he saw no reason why he should not use his position to encourage a wide enthusiasm for and participation in interests that were essentially private.

It was again a lack of judgement that led Nero into becoming something of a caricature of the imperial role which Seneca urged upon him. Thus *clementia* developed from a virtue designed to provide an acceptable basis for relations between himself and his subjects to one that became an attribute of a tyrannical monarch. It would be hard, however, to prove that Nero saw it as part of a process whereby the Roman principate was deliberately transformed into a Hellenistic monarchy.

Again, a lack of judgement may explain his attitude to other tendencies which might superficially be associated with Hellenistic monarchy. For example, his attitude to divinity may not have been born of a deliberate policy of self-apotheosis, but of extravagance and a perverse sense of theatre. It is not indeed beyond the bounds of possibility that 'Hellenistic features' in Nero's behaviour had a bearing on his desire to impose on the eastern part of the empire a recognition of his own domination; Caligula's construction of a 'bridge of boats' across the Bay of Naples may have been similarly motivated – and similarly ill judged.

Nero appears to have suffered from an immature and inadequate personality: the frantic striving for attention and the childlike frustration when he was disappointed suggest this. Many of his schemes show signs of escapism from a real world which he increasingly disliked; they also suggest, however, a determination to impose his will upon his contemporaries, whatever the cost. This is the sign of the megalomaniac, and ultimately the conception of the *domus aurea* represents the clearest physical expression of it. On 9 June AD 68, it was a megalomaniac and an inadequate man with Greek tastes who died, not a Hellenistic god–king.

5

Opposition and rebellion

During the early principate, there were three principal sources from which opposition to an emperor might surface – the imperial family itself, the senatorial order and the Praetorian Guard; only these groups had the standing and the access to force to enable them to succeed.

We have already seen (in Chapters 1 and 2) how intrigue within the imperial family managed Nero's rise to power, and then characterized the struggle for power between the new emperor and his mother which dominated the years between Nero's accession and his mother's murder. Events such as these were strongly reminiscent of similar struggles that had occupied Nero's Julio–Claudian predecessors. For its part, the Praetorian Guard remained loyal to Nero, initially because its commander was Afranius Burrus, one of the emperor's principal advisers. Latterly the same service was performed, although in a different manner, by the vicious Tigellinus. Only at the end did the loyalty of the praetorians waver when their last Neronian commander, Nymphidius Sabinus, accepted the promises of Galba's bribery to switch allegiance. At first, the senate, too, remained broadly content through Seneca's studied insistence on the 'Augustan ideal' as the model to be embraced by the young *princeps* under his charge.

This broadly based senatorial contentment remained intact until Nero's murder of his mother; even then many senators appear to have been persuaded by Seneca of the justification for the murder. One, however, was not prepared to merge into the silent majority: the name of Publius Clodius Thrasea Paetus, who had been *consul suffectus* in AD 56, is inextricably associated with the so-called 'stoic opposition' to Nero. In AD 59, he demonstrated his refusal to pass over the matricide by walking out of the senate, an act which Tacitus appears to diminish by suggesting that it opened Thrasea to danger without serving as a useful example to others – though it may have been a comment directed more at Thrasea's colleagues than at Thrasea himself.

What, then, was stoicism? It was a Greek philosophy which had been avidly embraced among Rome's upper classes; it was essentially a moral rather than a political philosophy, though Romans did not mark a clear distinction between morals and politics. Inevitably, in talking of virtue and duty it came to show how the moral man might serve the republic and keep intact his dignity and freedom. Its moral code made a strong appeal to traditionally minded Romans, and it came to be associated with *mos maiorum* ('ancestral custom'), that most traditional expression of morality and virtue. The turbulent politics of the late republic and early principate demonstrated a widening gulf between politics and morality; this might be said to have reached a new depth in Nero's murder of his mother. Because of its espousal of traditional virtues, stoicism in Rome came to be associated with the 'old republic' and with those who were perceived as its greatest champions – men such as Marcus Cato, who died in 46 BC, and Marcus Brutus, who died four years later.

Opposition to the emperor or the system was not obligatory upon stoics; Seneca, after all, managed to square his stoic beliefs with proximity to Nero, arguing perhaps that the next best thing to a 'philosopher–king' was a 'king' who was trained in the best governmental practices by a philosopher. Some stoics, however, thought differently, looking back for inspiration to the 'contests' between Caesar and Cato; even to contemporaries, like the historian Sallust, such a comparison was valid and powerful. Cicero, on the other hand, while he sometimes admired Cato's attachment to principles, could also dismiss him as cantankerous, cliquey and obsessive in propounding stances that were damaging to stable government. Cicero knew how Cato's intransigence, as much as anything, had forced the republic into civil war in 49 BC; he was made by Cato to feel an outsider in 'our struggle', but he also knew the destructive effect that Cato's suicide in 46 BC had on the balance which Caesar was trying to create. It was, after all, sufficient to bring Cicero himself to question where his true loyalties lay.

Thus eulogies of Cato and his friends became part of the hagiography of the spirit of the republic in its struggle with absolutism, though there was nothing in stoic doctrine that made such a stance inevitable; Brutus and Cassius, after all, were not stoics at all. Yet for some, Cato, Brutus and Cassius were brought together as the antitheses of autocracy. According to Tacitus, the Tiberian historian Cremutius Cordus made a speech extolling the blessings of *libertas*; in his history, Cordus had praised Brutus and referred to Cassius as 'the last of the Romans'. It was sufficient to provoke his death.

Tacitus remained ambivalent over the stoic politicians: both Thrasea and his son-in-law, the Elder Helvidius Priscus, are accused of glory-seeking. The Elder Helvidus went on to annoy even the patient Vespasian beyond redemption, conducting a campaign contrived to aggravate, insisting on addressing that *princeps* by his name rather than by his title. Further, Tacitus lived through what appears to have been the final denouement of this stoic group – the conspiracy of AD 93 against Domitian, led by Helvidius' son and coming as a culmination of such 'civil disobedience' as the composition of eulogistic biographies of Cato. Tacitus did not relish the outcome, but in the *Agricola* he shows that he realized how far such men (and women) contributed to their own downfalls:

> Let it be clear to those who insist on admiring insubordination that even under bad emperors men can be great, and that a decent regard for authority, if backed by ability and energy, can reach that peak of honour that many have stormed by precipitous paths, winning fame by a melodramatic death, but doing no service to their country.

An alternative, pragmatic, path is enshrined in the oration attributed to Galba, when in AD 69 the latter adopted Piso Licinianus as his son and successor (*Histories* I.15–16; Appendix I).

For Tacitus, as often for Cicero, the behaviour of the stoics was divorced from the real world and was a closed, cliquey affair. After all, many of the stoics of the Neronian and Flavian periods were related in a tight family group. Their doctrines were inopportune, as Tacitus shows in the case of the evangelical Musonius Rufus, who in AD 69 tried to preach the blessings of peace to those involved in civil war. Nor was it clear what they wanted, or upon what their objections were based. Did they want a different *princeps* or no *princeps*? Did they advocate a return to the old republic? Did they object to materialism, immorality – or to monarchy *per se*?

Thrasea Paetus, who came from northern Italy, said much of which Tacitus would clearly have approved, particularly when he was attacking corruption in government or the bending of the laws. But it was inevitable that a man who espoused older ideals and who, we may assume, will have approved of much, if not all, of the 'prospectus' which Seneca laid out for Nero in AD 54, should come into conflict with the emperor who, progressively from AD 59, seemed intent on forwarding the claims of a personal absolutism. For Thrasea, the deification of Poppaea and her infant daughter in AD 65 were as significant departures from tradition as Nero's murder of his mother.

Yet Thrasea was not a doctrinaire opponent of Nero nor, despite Tacitus' misgivings, did he take every opportunity for self-advertisement; during his trial for treason in AD 66 he refused to command an open stage, nor would he allow a younger friend, the tribune Arulenus Rusticus, to risk his life and career by interposing his veto on Thrasea's behalf. Much of what Thrasea said in the senate was moderate and sound, and calculated to expose corruption.

While relations between Nero and Thrasea Paetus had not been good since AD 59, we should still ask why it was that Nero determined on his destruction, along with that of Barea Soranus, in AD 66 in what Tacitus calls 'an assault upon Virtue itself'. Tacitus alleges that the trial was timed to coincide with the arrival in Rome of Tiridates to receive his diadem from Nero, in the hope that attention would be diverted from a 'domestic outrage', or possibly that Tiridates might regard it as a truly regal display of power.

The trial was clearly a ferocious affair: violent speeches of denunciation, encouraged by Nero, were made by Cossutianus Capito, Ostorius Sabinus and Eprius Marcellus, the first two of whom were clearly motivated by personal animosity against the defendants. The trial made much of the connection of attitude between Thrasea and his friends and Cato and of Thrasea's sometimes ostentatious disapproval of Nero's conduct:

> This is party warfare against the government. It is secession. If many more have the same impudence, it is war. As this faction-loving country once talked of Caesar versus Cato, so now, Nero, it talks of you versus Thrasea. And he has his followers – or his courtiers rather. They do not yet imitate his treasonable voting. But they copy his grim and gloomy manner and expression: they rebuke your amusements. He is the one man to whom your safety is immaterial, your talents unadmired. He dislikes the emperor to be happy. But even your unhappiness, your bereavements, do not appease him. Disbelief in Poppaea's divinity shows the same spirit as refusing allegiance to the acts of the divine Augustus and divine Julius. Thrasea rejects religion, abrogates law. In every province and army the official Gazette is read with special care – to see what Thrasea has refused to do. If his principles are better, let us adopt them. Otherwise, let us deprive these revolutionaries of their chief and champion.

The substance is hard to find; there is no indication that Thrasea at least had had any part in the conspiracy of Gaius Piso (see below) in the previous year; nor does Tacitus' account of it once mention him. Gaius Piso was personally a man of little consequence, and the motives of most of those involved are said to have been scarcely laudable. The only apparent stoic connection appears to have been provided by Seneca's nephew, the epic poet Lucan, whose motives for involvement were evidently personal, and who subsequently tried to excuse his own conduct by inculpating his mother. Seneca was subsequently required to end his life – perhaps a case of guilt by association.

However, while the driving force behind Piso's conspiracy may have been lightweight, there are signs that at the same time there was something more serious in the air. Tacitus writes of Gaius Piso's anxiety about the possibility of a rival claimant emerging in a descendant of Augustus named Lucius Junius Silanus Torquatus. Torquatus' name arises in a group of people who were punished in the months following Piso's conspiracy. Through this group a connection, however tenuous, emerges with Thrasea Paetus' co-defendant, Barea Soranus.

Barea was attacked by his accuser for his friendship with Rubellius Plautus, the descendant of Tiberius who, as we have seen, had earlier in the reign been accused of association with Agrippina. He had been forcibly retired from Rome, and then put to death in AD 62 on the instructions of Tigellinus. While the weakness of Plautus' position may have stemmed from his connections with Augustus and Tiberius, he may have had links that were politically more pertinent through his stoic connections. It prompts the suggestion that there was a network of people, some of whom had stoic associations, and some of whom may have been tempted into conspiracy.

Those whose punishments were recorded include Seneca's brother, Junius Gallio, and Anteius Rufus, a friend of Agrippina's who was probably related to Anteia, the wife of the younger Helvidius Priscus. Two suicides were ordered, those of Ostorius Scapula, the son of a Claudian governor of Britain and a friend of Anteius, and a man who was evidently feared by Nero, and of Antistius Vetus, the father-in-law of Rubellius Plautus. From this we *may* glean a connection between Rubellius Plautus and Domitius Corbulo; indeed, such was hinted at by Tigellinus when he persuaded Nero to have Plautus killed. Both Barea Soranus and Antistius Vetus had been proconsuls of Asia, while Corbulo was in the east. Further, Corbulo's daughter was married to Annius Vinicianus, whose father had participated in two plots against Claudius and whose brother, Annius Pollio, was the son-in-law of Barea Soranus. A conspiracy, attributed to a Vinicianus (presumably Corbulo's son-in-law) was detected at Beneventum in AD 66.

Corbulo himself was well connected through his mother, Vistilia, and it is possible that the general was married to a daughter of the blind jurist, Gaius Cassius Longinus, a descendant of Caesar's assassin. Cassius Longinus was one of those punished by Nero in the period after Piso's conspiracy: he was exiled, along with his wife's nephew, Lucius Junius Silanus Torquatus.

Thus although there was no apparent connection between the stoic group and those involved in Piso's conspiracy, Barea Soranus, at least, can be shown to have had links with men of prominent family, from some of whom the taint of conspiracy was not absent. There may indeed have been further connections with the Scribonius brothers, legates in the Germanies, whose suicides were required by Nero in AD 67 and whose associates, Sulpicius Camerinus and Licinius Crassus Frugi, also perished at this time.

These events may help to explain Nero's complaint against Barea Soranus; as a noted 'dissident', Thrasea Paetus may have been attacked by association rather than as a result of direct evidence. However, while Thrasea was evidently no conspirator, he was a man who stood for old-fashioned principles of conduct and deportment and whose dignity was impressive. Such adherence to tradition may have been sufficient to associate him in the emperor's eyes with some whose connections and beliefs rendered them more dangerous than Thrasea himself.

Ultimately, therefore, Thrasea was not a revolutionary; he had his opportunities to take or encourage dramatic action, but eschewed them. He, however, more than most reinforced the appearance of a connection between stoicism and republicanism, although in reality he did little more than to press, like Seneca, for an improvement of the present situation. It was both ironic and inevitable that he should himself become, like Cato, a luminary for future generations. For the increasingly extreme stance of the 'philosophical opposition' under the Flavians readily added Thrasea to its list of martyrs. In their different ways, Seneca and Thrasea demonstrated by their actions that there was no inherent inconsistency between stoicism and the principate; Nero's attack on Thrasea Paetus, however, ensured that this would change and that the descendants of Cato and Caesar were now set on a course of collision.

While Thrasea may have been determined to demonstrate a respect for the past which might offer hope for the future, others used Nero's growing absolutism and subsequent unpopularity as a pretext for the furthering of ambition: the course of Piso's conspiracy in AD 65 amply demonstrated this, along with the danger that an emperor who survived an attempt on his life might become more of a monster as a result, as he reflected upon such a manifestation of his subjects' lack of gratitude to him.

From first to last, aside from a few acts of individual honour and heroism, the conspiracy of Piso is shown by Tacitus to have been characterized by the cowardice and self-interest of most of its participants. There was little that was uplifting in the choice of Nero's 'successor', as Tacitus shows:

As soon as next year's consuls took office, a conspiracy was hatched and instantly gained strength. Senators and other gentry, officers, even women, competed to join. They hated Nero; and they liked Gaius Calpurnius Piso. His membership of the aristocratic Calpurnian house linked him, on his father's side, with many illustrious families. Among the masses, too, he enjoyed a great reputation for his good qualities, real or apparent. For he employed his eloquence to defend his fellow citizens in court; he was a generous friend – and gracious and affable even to strangers; and he also possessed the accidental advantages of impressive stature and a handsome face. But his character lacked seriousness or self-control. He was superficial, ostentatious, and sometimes dissolute. But many people are fascinated by depravity and disinclined for austere morals on the throne. Such men found Piso's qualities attractive. However, his ambitions were not what originated the conspiracy. Who did, who initiated this enterprise which so many joined, I could not easily say.

The historian proceeds to indicate a variety of motives for joining among the leading figures; a few are credited with patriotism, but most were stimulated by personal animosity or ambition. Most had reached the point where, for their own reasons, they found Nero's behaviour intolerable – whether it was his growing absolutism, supposed Hellenism or simply his personal treatment of them. The poet Lucan, for example, seems to have been motivated by nothing more than his poetic rivalry with the emperor. In such circumstances, the plot's failure was hardly surprising, and it stands as a fitting epitaph to an ill-conceived enterprise that, while men were falling over themselves to exculpate themselves, one of the few shining examples of courage and attachment to principle was provided by Epicharis, a former slave.

In his fear and frustration Nero ordered savage reprisals which, if anything, heightened the impression of his progress towards tyrannical absolutism. His escape was due, it was argued, to divine intervention: *Sol Invictus* ('the unconquerable Sun') had shed the light which had revealed the plot, while Jupiter Vindex sanctioned the emperor's revenge. As we have seen, contemporary coinage displayed the *princeps* as under Jupiter's guardianship and as the vice-gerent of the Sun. It was at the same time that the Colossus of Nero–Helios was erected outside the Golden House and Tiridates paid homage to Nero as Mithras, the divine vice-gerent of the Sun.

Tacitus' account suggests that Nero was almost paranoid as he suspected involvement on the part of all of his enemies; Seneca was required to commit suicide and, as we have seen, other deaths followed which might indicate either that the emperor's suspicions were now out of control, or that in the wake of the failed conspiracy, other, perhaps more serious attempts were made to bring the Julio–Claudian dynasty to an end – possibly involving highly placed military figures.

It provides evidence in any case that disenchantment – or, as Nero would have seen it, rejection and ingratitude – was now widespread. This disenchantment among highly placed Romans was clearly exacerbated by Nero's decision in AD 67 to mount his tour of Greece. Further, his absence, as the freedman Helius feared, offered the opportunity to members of the aristocracy to ponder and plan for action. As Tacitus notes, the dedication of the would-be assassin's dagger in AD 65 to Jupiter Vindex ('Jupiter the Avenger') turned out to be an omen, as pent-up frustration manifested itself in the rebellion initiated in Gaul in the spring of AD 68 by the governor of Gallia Lugdunensis, Gaius Julius Vindex.

6

The end of Nero: Galba,
Otho and Vitellius

Nero returned from his tour of Greece towards the end of AD 67; Helios had been urging this course of action upon him for some time. Up to AD 65, as we have seen, opposition had probably been more of a nuisance than a real threat to the stability of Nero's position, though the rebellion of Vinicianus in AD 66 may have been more serious if, as it appears, army-commanders were involved.

As we have seen (in Chapter 3), Nero's reaction was to reverse a policy of favouring the older nobility which had characterized the earlier part of the reign; instead, he appears to have placed in senior commands men whose social backgrounds might tempt them less to see themselves as potential rivals for Nero's power. While many such men were not wanting in energy, they may have lacked the *auctoritas* to maintain control when stability started to slip – a task made more difficult by Nero's evident failure to pay his armies the kind of attention that had been characteristic of most of his predecessors.

The source of the trouble which was to precipitate Nero's fall was the governor of the Gallic province of Lugdunensis, Gaius Julius Vindex, himself a Romanized Gaul. However, despite Vindex's origins and the inevitable comparison of his movement with the overtly nationalistic rebellion in AD 69 of another Romanized provincial, Gaius Julius Civilis, the coinage associated with Vindex's movement makes it clear that its objective was no more radical than the removal of Nero from power and his replacement by another *princeps*; it was *not* a nationalistic revolt aimed at removing the imperial power from Gaul. Tacitus assessed its true significance when he wrote: 'The secret of empire was out, that an emperor could be made elsewhere than at Rome.' In its turn, this demonstrates the vanity of the hope that Augustus' military reforms had brought to an end the politically disruptive power of the Roman army and its commanders, which had brought the old republic to its knees.

The details of Vindex's rebellion are in many particulars confused, as the versions in our extant sources are not entirely consistent. It appears, however, that late in AD 67 Vindex took an initiative by communicating with colleagues in the provinces to sound them out regarding their attitude to Nero. The responses were evidently mostly equivocal, and some appear to have informed Nero. That Nero did not make any dramatic counter-moves at that stage is not, however, surprising: Vindex's province was not armed and his status was questionable. In any case Nero will have believed that the legions on the Rhine, under Lucius Verginius Rufus and Gaius Fonteius Capito, and in Spain, under Servius Sulpicius Galba, were more than sufficient to deal with any rebellion that might erupt in western Europe.

Vindex declared his rebellion in mid-March, probably to coincide with the Ides (15th) and its association with Caesar's assassination (which was actually recalled in a coin issue) and the anniversary of Agrippina's murder (19th). His objections to Nero centred largely around the matricide and the emperor's unbecoming conduct – that is, his Hellenism. The figurehead for Vindex's movement was the governor of Tarraconensis (in Spain), Servius Galba, who was supported by his neighbour in Lusitania, Marcus Salvius Otho (the former friend of Nero), and by three legionary commanders – Titus Vinius (in Tarraconensis), and Fabius Valens and Caecina Alienus (on the Rhine). Nonetheless, Galba was circumspect in his own actions, and on 2 April declared himself 'legate of the senate and people of Rome', evidently hesitating concerning an outright bid for supreme power. A short-lived complication in the west was the *apparently* independent rebellion by Lucius Clodius Macer, commander of the legion in Africa, who, of course, had the power to cut grain supplies from his province.

The chief difficulty, however, was posed by Lucius Verginius

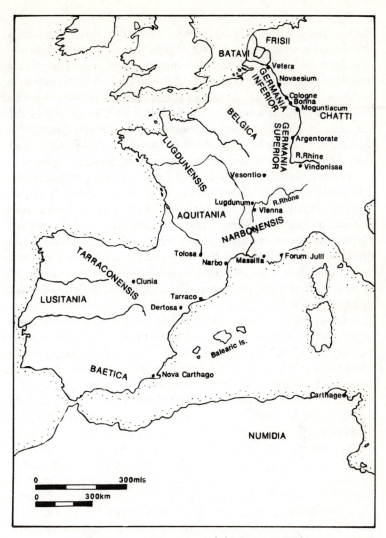

4. The Western Provinces of the Roman Empire

Rufus, governor of Upper Germany, whose responsibility it should have been to deal with 'Gallic brush fires'. Verginius' colleague in Lower Germany, Fonteius Capito, was evidently hostile to Vindex and Galba, though too distant for immediate action in this instance. Although it is unclear what view Verginius Rufus took personally of the rebellion of Vindex and Galba – and there is some evidence to suggest sympathy – it is certain that his soldiers, when mobilized in March of AD 68, were clear that their job was to defend the emperor against his enemies.

Suetonius indicates that it was Galba's open entry into the fray (on 2 April) that first caused Nero anxiety; the early moves had apparently given him so little worry that, on his return from Greece, he had left Rome almost immediately – this time for Naples, the nearest equivalent to Greece perhaps that Italy could offer. Suetonius describes Nero breaking into a tantrum – not uncommon when he felt that he had been shown a lack of gratitude – but he then organized a military line of defence based upon the river Po.

In the event, however, this line of defence was not called upon to act, for in May – the precise date is uncertain – the legions of Upper Germany clashed with Vindex's troops at Vesontio (Besançon); Vindex's troops were massacred and he himself committed suicide. The whole venture had turned sour, for it would appear that Vindex had relied upon *not* having to fight the German legions and had evidently been negotiating with Verginius Rufus to avoid it. The clash had occurred contrary to the wishes of the two commanders. Although the German army's victory might have saved Nero's throne for him, the soldiers then extraordinarily offered to desert Nero if Verginius himself would accept power. He declined, arguing that power lay properly in the hands of the senate and people, although the news that reached Nero evidently convinced him that he could not now count on the legions of the Rhine. Tacitus says that Nero was really defeated by rumours rather than by real defections, and this seems to stem from the fact that he failed to understand that Verginius' refusal of his soldiers' offer left them one option only – to return to their earlier allegiance. It is also likely that Verginius refused not out of a positive regard for constitutionalism (as was subsequently claimed by his friends), but because, sickened by the outcome of Vesontio, he had resolved to take no further part in these events.

Following Vesontio the Praetorian Guard in Rome withdrew its support from Nero, induced it seems by bribes offered to it in the name of Galba by its commander, Nymphidius Sabinus. Soon after, the senate turned against Nero and declared for Galba; Nero left Rome, and on 9 June committed suicide.

Nero's death brought the Julio–Claudian line to its end, and power had passed by a military revolt, organized by members of the senatorial aristocracy, to Galba, an elderly man, living on the laurels of a distinguished career and descended from a patrician family of old nobility. Galba himself had enjoyed favour from the Julio–Claudian house, in particular from Livia, the wife of Augustus and mother of Tiberius.

Galba proved to be a martinet, with old-fashioned ideas of probity, but ironically totally unable to exercise any control over his closest entourage. He was seen as a man who forced on others the morality of an earlier generation, but who himself lived in a court distinguished by its inefficiency and corruption. In other words, he could hardly carry conviction for firm government. He allowed his favourites a free rein while he himself exacerbated the sensibilities of various groups by his harsh treatment of political opponents, by his decision to recoup to the state many of Nero's gifts and by refusing to pay the donatives promised in his name to the Praetorian Guard. Against this, his public message proclaimed through the coinage of Concord, Restored Liberty and the Rebirth of Rome appeared marginal and irrelevant.

His inconsistencies were probably the most immediate cause of his downfall after only a few months as *princeps*. His attitude to opponents was little short of paranoia: many of those who had failed to support his cause in 68 were bloodily removed or at best disgraced, and were replaced by weak men whom Galba presumably saw as posing no threat to him. These replacements however proved incapable of exercising a reasoned discipline when this was required; his appointments to the two German army groups typified this: one, Hordeonius Flaccus, elderly and gout-ridden, the other, Aulus Vitellius, the possessor of an impressive pedigree but little else. Galba's problems were further exacerbated by the fact that he was seen as ungrateful by those who had helped him during 68. Two of the German legionary commanders, Valens and Caecina, and Marcus Salvius Otho were evidently expecting tangible signs of

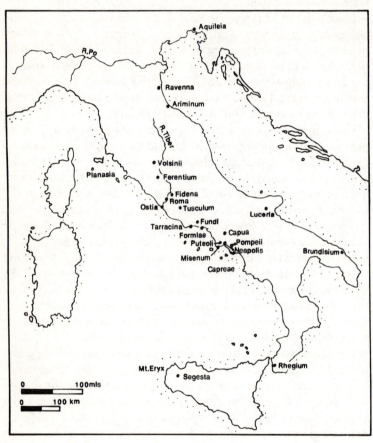

5. Italy

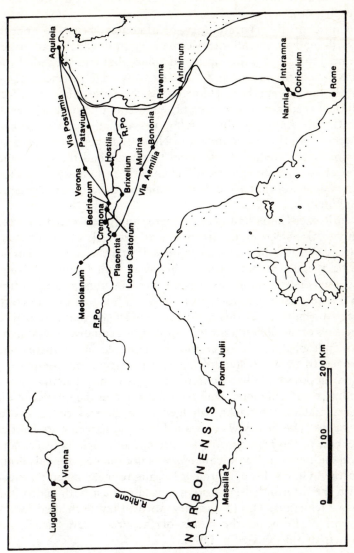

6. Northern Italy, AD 69

Galba's gratitude, which were not forthcoming. Similarly the Praetorian Guard felt badly let down by Galba's refusal to pay the donative which had been promised in return for their treachery to Nero.

Consequently separate areas of discontent began to appear. By the end of AD 68 the German legions, which had never wanted to accept Galba in the first place, but had yielded to the persuasion of Valens and Caecina, now felt justified, again under their persuasion, to throw off their allegiance. In effect all they needed was a respectable candidate to put up as a rival to Galba; Aulus Vitellius, who, despite an undistinguished career – latterly as a confidant of Nero – had been appointed by Galba to the command of Lower Germany, had the status and was chosen as the figurehead. Thus early in January AD 69 the German legions put aside their allegiance to Galba and declared for Vitellius.

In Rome, Galba had become increasingly convinced that the only real objection to his rule was his lack of an obvious successor. Otho had convinced himself that the role was bound to be assigned to him. Instead, however, Galba chose a blameless but sombre young aristocrat, Piso Licinianus, and according to Tacitus, used the moment to deliver a 'manual of statecraft' (see Appendix I). In this Galba acknowledged that a return to the days of the old republic was impossible; equally, however, the principle of dynastic succession inaugurated by Augustus had proved to be a disaster in that it was responsible for putting Nero in power. Galba's compromise was to find a man of good pedigree and character, who would command the respect of his peers and thus be acknowledged by a general consensus as *princeps*. The theory was reasonable – and indeed bore fruit at the end of the first century AD in emperors such as Nerva and Trajan; however, Piso Licinianus was not the man for this hour. Further, Otho's disappointment led him to make common cause with the disgruntled Praetorian Guard to oust both Galba and Piso Licinianus. On 15 January AD 69 they both died in the streets of Rome at the hands of the Praetorian Guard; the principate thus passed to Otho.

Otho's elevation fanned the flames of the German legionary rebellion. Otho was not their choice and was totally unacceptable to them in so far as he had been chosen by the Praetorian Guard; rivalry between the praetorians and the legions was not a new phenomenon. The praetorians were envied for their pay and conditions of service and detested for their elitism. Thus Vitellius, originally elevated as a rival to Galba, was now retained as a rival to Otho and the Praetorian Guard. Another emerging feature of these months was the *esprit de corps* of the various army groups; as Vitellius' campaign against Otho developed, so other army groups contemplated candidates of their own, or expressed a preference for Otho or Vitellius. Thus the British legions joined Vitellius, while those of the Danube and east preferred Otho. It was in such a context of rivalry between various army groups that the wishful thinking of coin issues proclaiming 'the Harmony of the Armies' became relevant.

Although Otho's reputation as governor of Lusitania had been good, he was generally thought of as idle and self-indulgent; indeed Tacitus saw the main problems of his short-lived principate as deriving from a need to live down this reputation and from the task (regarded by Tacitus as of impossible immensity) of undoing the harm done to the concept of loyalty by his murder of Galba. Tacitus did not believe that future loyalty could be built upon such an act of disloyalty.

In his campaign against Vitellius, Otho displayed both courage and determination. In addition he was able to attract subordinate officers of good standing, such as Marius Celsus and Suetonius Paullinus. Perhaps his most striking quality, however, was the personal magnetism that he exercised over his troops. His chief problem was logistical: Vitellius was attacking Italy with considerable numbers of the best legionary troops in the empire, while Otho had to hand only the Praetorian Guard and some relatively inexperienced legionaries. Although the legions of the Danubian and eastern provinces were pledged to support him, few of these had any hope of reaching Italy in time to participate in an early campaign.

For Otho, speed was of the essence; the Vitellian troops were approaching Italy in two groups, and Otho's only realistic hope was to be able to take them on separately. Herein lay his dilemma: Otho's troops were eager for an early battle, but his commanders were for waiting for the arrival of reinforcements. Their delaying tactics were interpreted by the troops as evidence of planned treachery. Otho made a further mistake in his decision not to accompany his troops in their front-line positions at Placentia, on the river Po, but to stay in a rearward position (at Brixellum) to exercise overall supervision and to keep command of the road into Italy from the east. In the event, a battle was fought at Bedriacum on the north side of the river, which Otho's troops lost – but not disastrously. By now, however, morale was sliding, and in an act of self-sacrificing courage Otho decided to commit suicide to prevent further bloodshed. Ironically, the first reinforcements arrived from the Danube soon afterwards.

Thus in mid-April of AD 69 Rome had in Aulus Vitellius her third emperor since Nero's death only ten months previously. Like Otho's, Vitellius' reputation was built largely on his association with Nero's more self-indulgent pursuits; unlike Otho, however, Vitellius did little in his principate to rise above this reputation. He remained self-indulgent, and his actions divisive. For example, the deliberate humiliation which he inflicted on the legions from the Danube which had come to fight for Otho in making them rebuild amphitheatres in Cremona, followed by their unceremonious despatching back to the Danube, left them angry and eager for revenge. Otho's Praetorian Guard was disbanded and replaced by soldiers from the Rhine legions, keen to sample the opportunities offered by well-paid jobs in Italy; the Rhine legions were brought back to strength with raw recruits, which was to have dangerous consequences later in the year. Further, Vitellius' victorious troops treated Italy as if it were the conquered victim in a foreign war, ripe for plunder.

Under such circumstances it was scarcely likely that the Roman world would settle to loyalty to the new *princeps*. The legions of the Danube provinces, who were most aggrieved at their treatment by Vitellius, had no candidate of sufficient seniority to stand as a rival to him but did find a leader of drive and energy in Antonius Primus, the commander of legion VII. He persuaded the Danubian legions to make common cause with the legions of the east who did have a reputable candidate in Titus Flavius Vespasianus (Vespasian), the governor of Judaea, who had won a strong military reputation in the ongoing Jewish war. The strength of his position lay in the fact that, as a result of the efforts of his elder son (the future emperor, Titus), he had buried his political and personal differences with Licinius Mucianus, the governor of Syria. Thus all the eastern legions and their commanders were able to make common cause under Vespasian's banner.

Of course, this impressive army from the Danube and the east could not in its entirety reach Italy quickly. However, a first wave moved under Antonius Primus, with a second following behind under Mucianus. Vespasian himself made a longer journey through Egypt to gather funds, and presumably to put himself in a position to threaten Italy's grain supply, much of which came from Egypt. Tacitus' account of his journey indicates that it was important from the point of view of Vespasian's 'image-makers' for, as a first-generation senator who was the son of an equestrian tax collector, he could hardly be said to have enjoyed a standing that matched those of descendants of the old republican nobility (such as the Julio–Claudians and Galba) or even those of Augustan ennoblement (such as Otho and Vitellius).

Vitellius' troops, while impressive 'on paper', were in a low state of morale due to their undisciplined lifestyle in Italy, but to prevent any chance that they might be reinforced from Germany, Antonius Primus arranged for a diversion on the Rhine in the shape of a 'rebellion' headed by two Romanized Batavians, Julius Civilis and Julius Classicus. In the event this went right out of hand, and in the midst of her civil war Rome found herself with a dangerous nationalist rebellion which almost brought the Rhine garrison to its knees before it was eventually repulsed. Further, little help was forthcoming from the Vitellian stronghold of Britain, since the British army was similarly occupied with a rebellion in the north which brought to an end the long-standing arrangement with the pro-Roman queen, Cartimandua, of the Brigantes.

Vitellius' discomfiture was compounded by the poverty of his command structure in Italy; his best commander, Fabius Valens, was too ill to participate, while the remaining commander, Caecina Alienus, was a man to whom, according to Tacitus, treachery was second nature. Even before the true onset of hostilities, Caecina was in negotiation with agents of Vespasian – which demoralized Vitellius' troops still further.

Vespasian's battle plan was for Antonius Primus to await the arrival of Mucianus in northern Italy for a joint assault on Vitellius' positions on the river Po. But Primus, wishing to strike while Vitellius' troops were in a poor state of morale and short of reinforcements, and anxious to avoid the worst of the autumn weather as he struck southwards for Rome, would not wait. Without doubt, it was an element in his decision to seek battle that he wished to defeat Vitellius' troops on the Po and reach Rome before Mucianus could join him, and so share the glory.

The Vitellians were defeated at a second battle in that year at Bedriacum, and Primus let loose the Danubian legions on the town of Cremona to avenge the disgrace that they had suffered there at Vitellius' hands earlier in the year. Events in Rome were chaotic as the Flavian troops moved in; there were rumours of Vitellius' abdication. But his decision to set fire to the temple of Jupiter on the Capitoline Hill and the murder of Vespasian's brother, Flavius Sabinus, put an end to any prospect of negotiation. On 20 December, Rome fell to Antonius Primus; Vitellius was arrested and put to death; Vespasian's younger son, Domitian, was hailed as 'Caesar'. Mucianus reached Rome at the very end of the month, and on 1 January AD 70 Rome saw a new reigning dynasty, the Flavian, inaugurated, with Vespasian and his elder son, Titus, as consuls for the new year.

Conclusion

In a period of eighteen months, the Julio–Claudian dynasty had been brought to a violent end and the power of the army and its commanders had reasserted itself as a political force; during this time there had been serious talk of the dangers of dynastic government, and yet the period had finished with the triumph of Vespasian and the opening of a new dynasty.

How far can responsibility for the collapse of the Julio–Claudian dynasty be ascribed to Nero himself? It is clear that many – particularly senators – found Nero's autocracy oppressive and unacceptable. After a favourable beginning, he had overstepped the Augustan principles with which he set out and was behaving in a manner which not only offended against those principles, but also against a broader range of traditionalist sentiment. This undoubtedly turned against him many who might otherwise have suffered in silence. It was this broad disenchantment within the senatorial order which prompted some senators to look again at the option of *military* rebellion which Augustus had appeared to foreclose after the battle of Actium. Nero's lack of interest in his armies and his treatment of some of its commanders during his later years had fuelled this disenchantment.

Yet it is evident that Nero's unpopularity was not universal; the later appearance of 'false Nero figures' suggests this, as does Galba's warning to Piso Licinianus, his proposed successor, that there would be some of his subjects who would be missing Nero. Nero's patronage of ordinary people, particularly in the matter of building work and entertainment, left a strong impression and provides an echo of the divided reactions to the murder of Caesar a century earlier. It is notable that only a few in the crisis of AD 68 – or indeed on previous similar occasions – contemplated the removal of the principate as a governing system. Of course, by AD 68 there were far fewer men in high places who had direct family connections with the old republic than had been the case, for example, when Augustus died in AD 14. While some of the propaganda of AD 68, evidenced in the coinage, reflected republican themes, most of it suggested that any 'new start' should take Augustan principles as its foundation.

Thus Nero can be seen to have done little damage to the principate as an institution, but his behaviour did raise questions about dynasticism and it would be difficult – if not impossible – to turn the clock back on the reappearance of the military as a *political* force. The general acceptability of the principate, however, had much to do with its reception among the mass of the population and in the provinces; Nero's positive contributions in these fields were not inconsiderable. Disquiet among members of the senatorial order and in the army bore most heavily on the fate of individual emperors, rather than on the system itself.

In the height of crisis therefore at the beginning of AD 69 we find Galba talking of ways in which the reality of the principate could be brought into harmony with traditionalist sentiment. It is evident that on this occasion, as again in not dissimilar circumstances after Domitian's death in AD 96, the chief concern was that adherence to a dynastic principle of imperial succession could not be relied upon to produce a sound ruler. Nero had provided good evidence that an emperor elevated according to a dynastic principle was likely to be capricious in his behaviour and overbearing and arrogant in his manner. Indeed Nero's behaviour seems to have had much in common with an attitude ascribed to Caligula – that he was 'untouchable' because he was 'born to rule'.

Galba advocated the choice of the best man available as the means by which a sounder principate might emerge. However, the events of AD 68–69 showed clearly the pressures militating against such an approach. In the first place, in AD 68 some of the legions, despite Nero's lack of interest in them, were diffident of deserting him. As Tacitus observed, Nero was unseated more by rumours of rebellion than by rebellion itself. However, the successful elevation of Galba as a result of military rebellion brought new pressures to bear: an emperor who rises by rebellion inevitably has debts to settle and is likely to be plagued by the fear that what he has done could be repeated by another. As in Galba's case, this led to a reluctance to utilize the services of men whose strength could conceivably make them a political threat. Further, faced with the resultant weak leadership, armies rapidly devised agendas of their own which had much more to do with their own short-term advantages than with the good of Rome and the empire. The reality of this was vividly and violently illustrated by the totally irresponsible way in which Vespasian's agent, Antonius Primus, stirred up a tribal uprising on the Rhine purely as a diversionary tactic to occupy the legions supporting Vitellius. The result of this was a near disaster.

Since Augustus had made the army permanent and placed it in strategic frontier dispositions, long periods of duty in the same locations had fostered the development of local, or group, loyalties. Thus rebellions could be mounted so that one army group might display its muscle or get its own back on another group. Such an attitude was particularly evident in the behaviour of the Rhine legions supporting Vitellius: they first raised a rebellion against Galba because they had never wanted him, and they then continued it after Galba's death because they had not chosen Otho and because the new emperor was supported by the Praetorian Guard, members of which they hated as elitist and over-privileged.

Clearly, to be successful and stable, any candidate for power who emerged as a result of a military rebellion had to be firm, disciplined, constructive and conciliatory. Galba never displayed such attributes, while Otho showed that he understood the need of them but never had the backing to establish himself securely. The self-indulgent Vitellius seems not to have given such matters the merest thought.

At the beginning of AD 70, therefore, there was a great burden on the shoulders of Vespasian if he was to establish successfully the power he had won in civil war. In the event, he showed no fear of making radical changes in crucial areas – legionary

81

dispositions, organization of auxiliary units of the Roman army, and controlling the army's command structure in the interests of himself and the state. He saw the need too of the reconstruction and conciliation that had characterized Augustus after Actium. However, as a first-generation senator, he lacked the personal *auctoritas* associated with aristocratic Julians and Claudians. The 'image-makers' went to work, associating Vespasian with such events as 'healing miracles', but Vespasian's major contribution to the creation of an image was his indication from the start that he was founding a new dynasty – the Flavian.

He issued coinage in the name of his two sons, Titus and Domitian, who both took the name Caesar into their nomenclatures. He even experimented with making Titus prefect of the Praetorian Guard. He established his dynasty's broadly based acceptability though patronage – work, food and entertainment for the masses, and advancement for those men of the senatorial and equestrian orders who were seen to merit it. Opposition was largely confined to a group of stoics, who were much more extreme in their attitudes during the Flavian period than they had been under Nero; perhaps it took extremism to oppose Vespasian who was the one and only emperor of the first century AD whom Tacitus admitted to have been changed for the better by his exercise of supreme power.

The Flavian dynasty ran its course: Titus succeeded his father (AD 79–81), and was succeeded in turn by his younger brother, Domitian (AD 81–96). Many members of the senatorial order recognized in the new dynasty a similar deterioration to that which had overtaken the Julio–Claudians. Thus the death of Domitian in AD 96 was precipitated and followed by pressures and preoccupations that were remarkably reminiscent of those that surrounded the fall of the last of the Julio–Claudians.

APPENDIX I

Galba's speech to Piso on the latter's adoption as successor (Tacitus Histories, I.15–16)

Tacitus provides what purports to be the text of a speech which Galba made on 10 January AD 69 on the occasion of his adoption of Lucius Calpurnius Piso Frugi Licinianus as his son and successor. It is doubtful whether a text of such a speech survived which Tacitus could have consulted, although he could no doubt have gained an impression of it from people who heard it. It is however more likely that, as with the speech of Claudius in AD 48 on the admission of Gallic aristocrats to senatorial membership, Tacitus has followed the maxim of the Athenian Thucydides in producing his own version of the speech, encapsulating 'sentiments appropriate to the occasion'.

The purpose of the speech in Tacitus' narrative has been much discussed, and by some it has been regarded as a 'manual of statecraft', laying out Tacitus' own principles of government under the principate. Because of this it has been argued that the speech has less to do with events in the mid-first century AD than with Tacitus' own times – in particular, the confused and dangerous events of the principate of the aged Nerva in AD 96–98, which culminated in that emperor's adoption of Trajan as his son and successor.

At the least, however, the 'dramatic date' of Galba's oration provides an opportunity for comment on the system of government under the Julio–Claudians – particularly with regard to the dynastic principle itself. It also offers in passing a *senatorial*

83

view on the reign of Nero; as with other emperors however – most notably perhaps Domitian (AD 81–96) – it is as well to remember that the senatorial viewpoint, because of the circumstances of the relationship between emperors and the senate, might present a set of opinions markedly different from those entertained by other sections of the community.

'If I were a private citizen, adopting you in the presence of the priests according to time-honoured formalities, I should content myself with dwelling on the great honour it does my family to bring into it a man who has the blood of Gnaeus Pompeius and Marcus Crassus in his veins; for your part, you would feel similarly gratified at the opportunity to link your own noble family with my roots in the families of the Sulpicii and the Lutatii. As it is, however, it is by the unanimous consent of gods and men that I am emperor; thus it is your outstanding qualities of character and your patriotism that prompt me in a time of peace to offer to you a principate for which our ancestors – and indeed I myself – had to take up arms.

'I am conscious of the example of the deified Augustus, who raised a series of men to a position of power second only to his own – first, his sister's son, Gaius Claudius Marcellus, then his son-in-law, Marcus Agrippa; later still he promoted his grandsons, Gaius and Lucius Caesar, and finally his stepson, Tiberius Claudius Nero. Augustus confined his search for a successor to his family, whilst I have extended mine to the whole state; this is not because I have no close relations or army colleagues. My acceptance of the imperial power was not driven by my sense of ambition, and it would be taken as an indication that I have exercised my judgement that, in choosing you, I have passed over not just my relatives, but yours too. You have a brother, as noble in birth as you, and older; he would be worthy of this honour, were you not a better choice.

'You are old enough to have left youthful enthusiasm behind, and you have nothing in your past life which requires excuse. Until now, you have had only misfortunes to bear; success tests the human spirit more critically. This is because we bear misfortune, whilst success corrupts us. Loyalty, independence and friendship represent the outstanding qualities of the human character; you have maintained your grasp on these with great determination, and will continue to do so. Others, however, will seek to undermine them through their sycophancy. You will be assaulted by flattery, by specious arguments, and by individual self-interest, which inflict the greatest damage on sincere relationships. You and I today can talk straightforwardly to each other on a personal basis; others, however, will be more ready to treat us as emperors than as human beings. Advising an emperor on the right course of action is an act of real commitment, whilst agreeing with everything an emperor says is accomplished with no real affection.

'If this extensive empire of ours could remain stable without a ruler, I would consider it an achievement to be able to reestablish the old republic. As it is, it long ago came to the point where, as I grow older, I cannot do the Roman people a better service than to give them a good successor, whilst your greatest gift to them in your youth will be to give them a good emperor. In the reigns of Tiberius, Gaius (Caligula) and Claudius, Rome was effectively the heirloom of a single family; thus my introduction of the principle of choice will represent a move towards liberty. Now that the Julian and Claudian dynasty has reached its end, the choice of the best emperor will be made by the process of adoption. To be born of emperors is a matter of pure chance and is not valued more highly than that; the act of adoption implies an exercise of unimpeded judgement, and if one wishes, the choice is confirmed by public consensus.

'Let Nero's example remain before your eyes; he vaunted himself as the last of a long line of Caesars. It was not Vindex with an unarmed province or I myself with a single legion that brought him down and freed the Roman people from the burden of him; it was his own excesses and luxurious wastefulness. Nor was there at that time any precedent for an emperor suffering such a condemnation. We won the power through arms and because we were thought right for the job; but no matter how outstanding our performance, we shall become the targets of envy. Do not feel threatened because two legions have not yet recovered their equilibrium after the great convulsion that the empire has seen; my accession was not untroubled, and once news of your adoption spreads I shall cease to seem old – which has been the only objection that could be levelled at me. Nero will always be missed by the worst elements of society; it is our job – yours and mine – to make sure that men of quality do not come to miss him too.

'This is not the occasion for more extended advice; indeed all necessary precautions are in place if I have done a good job in choosing you. The quickest and simplest test of right and wrong is for you to consider what actions you would approve or criticize if someone else were emperor. Rome is not like those countries which are ruled by kings, and in which everyone is a slave to the ruling house; you are about to become emperor amongst a people who can handle neither serfdom nor uncontrolled freedom.'

Appendix II

Nero's Golden House

The fullest account in antiquity is to be found in Suetonius' *Life of Nero* (section 31):

'The most wasteful of all his activities was his building programme: he built a house which stretched from the Palatine to the Esquiline, which he called the *domus transitoria*. When it was later burnt down he rebuilt it with the new name, *domus aurea*. The following details will provide some idea of its size and opulence: at its entrance way, there stood the *Colossus*, a statue of himself which was 120 feet high; so spacious was the site that there was a triple colonnade running for a whole mile. There was a lake which was so large that it resembled the sea, and was surrounded by buildings which were constructed to look like whole cities; moreover, there were rustic areas which were landscaped with ploughed fields, vineyards, pastures and woods, in which great herds of every kind of domestic and wild animal roamed around.

'In the house itself, all surfaces were covered with gold leaf, and encrusted with precious stones and pearls; the dining rooms had fretted ceilings fitted with panels of ivory which were movable and equipped with pipes so that flower petals and perfumes could be showered on those below. The main dining room took the form of a *rotunda* which revolved day and night in synchronization with the heavens. The baths had a constant supply of sea water and water from sulphurous springs. When the decoration of the house had been completed in this fashion Nero dedicated it, adding approvingly that he could now at last begin to live like a human being.'

Tacitus (*Annals* XV.42) confirms that the designers, Severus and Celer, were masters of mechanical wizardry. For a description and plan, see A. Boethius and J.B. Ward-Perkins, *Etruscan and Roman Architecture*, London 1970 (pp. 214–16); A.G. MacKay, *Houses, Villas and Palaces in the Roman World*, London 1975 (pp. 128–31).

APPENDIX III

Glossary of Latin terms

Auctoritas: This concept, which was central to the Augustan principate, is hard to render precisely; it means 'influence' and 'prestige', and embraces the idea of acquiring these through a combination of heredity, wealth, personality and achievement. Importantly, it implies the ability to patronize on a large scale.

Clementia: This means 'clemency', or being sparing to political adversaries: while it might on particular occasions be welcome in its effects, in principle it was a 'virtue' related to men of overwhelming (and thus unwelcome) power, which could be denied as capriciously as it was exercised.

Colonia: A city founded deliberately with a hand-picked population of Roman citizens, who were intended to act as a military 'reserve' and as overseers of the neighbouring local population with a view to 'Romanizing' it. This 'duty' was compensated by the allowance of a certain degree of self-regulation of affairs. The planting of *coloniae* had a long history in the growth of Roman power in Italy and beyond, and was used during the principate as a way of settling legionary veterans in sensitive areas. It differed from a *municipium* which was a status involving a grant of citizen rights to an *existing* population.

Consul: The *consul* was the head of the executive branch of government during the republic; two were elected each year, and were accountable to the electorate for their tenure of office. They presided over meetings of the senate and assemblies of the *populus* (whole people), and regularly commanded the armies in battle until the late third century BC, when this function was increasingly taken over by promagistrates (*proconsul, propraetor*). Under the principate, while prestige still attached to the office, its importance came to relate more to the provincial and army commands for which it represented a 'qualification'. Also under the principate it became normal for the consuls who took office on 1 January (*ordinarii*), and who gave their names to the year, to resign midway through the year in favour of replacements (*consules suffecti*). This was a method of increasing the numbers of men qualified for senior commands.

Cursus honorum: The ladder of offices climbed during the republic by senators in their quest for the consulship. It was subject to a number of organizing laws (e.g. the Lex Villia of 180 BC, and Lex Cornelia of Sulla), which laid down intervals between offices as well as the proper order for holding them. Under the principate the *cursus* remained in place, though a man's progress along it was affected by imperial favour (or the lack of it), and by the number of his legitimate children. The chief offices under the principate (and ages of tenure) were:

Vigintivirate (board of twenty)	18
Military tribune	21–22
Quaestor	25
Tribune of the plebs (often omitted)	
Aedile (often omitted)	
Praetor	30–35
Legionary commander (*legatus legionis*)	30+
Consul	37+
Proconsul or *legatus Augusti*	38+

Dictator: Originally an office held for six months in an emergency, both consuls having agreed to abdicate. Sulla and Caesar, however, had longer tenures and used the office and the protections it gave (e.g. freedom from tribunician veto) as the basis of a permanent control of government.

Dignitas: This 'dignity' referred specifically to the holding of offices of the *cursus honorum*. It was, for example, an affront to Caesar to be barred from competing for a second consulship, which by 50 BC he was entitled to do. Similarly Tiberius took it as an affront to his *dignitas* that in 6 BC he was given tribunician power simply to annoy Gaius and Lucius Caesar.

Dominatio: The state of being a master (*dominus*): the word originally and properly referred to the state of being a master of slaves, but it was increasingly used to describe the position and behaviour of Julius Caesar and (by some) of Augustus.

Equites: Members of the equestrian order during the principate were Rome's second social class. Originally a rather disparate body, the order acquired coherence through its commercial activities following the expansion of empire from the second century BC. Companies formed within the order (*societates*) undertook (for profit) many tasks during the republic of a civil service nature. Augustus reorganized the order so that it had a career structure in which it carried out similar tasks, but for salaries rather than profits.

Imperium: The executive *power* bestowed on consuls and praetors during the republic, through which they 'controlled' the state. *Imperium* was tenable as it was defined – consular or proconsular. Augustus under the First Settlement controlled Gaül, Spain and Syria under a proconsular *imperium*, which was enhanced to superiority over others (*maius*) under the Second Settlement. He had a permanent 'residual' *imperium* which could be temporarily redefined to enable him to undertake other tasks, such as censorial duties.

Imperator: The word means 'general', and was used during the republic; it was used in the titulature of emperors to indicate their tenure of *imperium* and their 'superior generalship'. It was abbreviated to *IMP* on inscriptions and on the coinage.

Legatus: Originally a man to whom 'assistant' power was delegated; Pompey, for example, conducted his eastern campaigns with a number of *legati* in attendance. Under the principate a man became a *legatus* of a legion after the praetorship, but the term was usually employed of those to whom the emperor delegated *de facto* control of his provinces (*legatus Augusti pro praetore*), where the term 'pro praetore' was used of ex-consuls in order visibly to subordinate them to the emperor's proconsular *imperium*.

Lex: A law, which had been passed either by one of the assemblies (*comitia*) of the whole people (*populus*), or by

91

the assembly of the plebeians (**concilium plebis**). Under the principate, the participation of these bodies became a mere formality.

Libertas: 'Freedom' had a wide collection of meanings at Rome, though that most frequently mentioned was the traditional *freedom* of the nobility to progress along the **cursus honorum** without undue interference from others. It was this *libertas* which was seen as being in conflict particularly with the principle of hereditary succession.

Municipium: see above, under *colonia*.

Nobilis: Literally, one who was 'known'; the *nobiles* (aristocracy) defined themselves as deriving from families who had reached the consulship in earlier generations, and regarded the consulship as virtually their birthright.

Optimates: The *optimates* (or self-styled 'best men') during the republic were those *nobiles* who felt that their factional dominance should be exercised primarily through an influential senate taking the leading role in government. It was effectively the *optimates*, with their blinkered view of Rome and its empire, who forced Caesar and Pompey to war in 49 BC and who were central in Caesar's assassination five years later. During Augustus' reign they and their descendants found the family of the Claudii a more suitable rallying point than that of the Julii.

Pater patriae: An honorific title, 'father of the country': it was awarded to Cicero in 63 BC for his defeat of Catiline's conspiracy, and was held by Roman emperors after it had been given to Augustus in 2 BC.

Patrician: Traditionally the oldest part of Rome's aristocracy who in the republic's early days exercised the decisive role in government, maintaining a stranglehold through law and patronage over the political, military, legal and religious machinery of the state. The 'struggle of the orders' (trad. 509–287 BC) gave more equality to *rich* plebeians, so that the real effectiveness of the distinction between the classes was eroded. Subsequently the main factional groups (*optimates* and *populares*) each contained members of both classes. Augustus tried to revive the patriciate as the central core of his patronized aristocracy. Patricians were debarred from holding plebeian offices, such as the tribunate of the plebs and the plebeian aedileship.

Pietas: The 'sense of duty' to gods, state and family which represented the traditional loyalties of the Roman noble and which Augustus tried to exemplify and revitalize.

Populares: The term, meaning 'mob-panderers', was coined by the *optimates* to describe the way in which their opponents appeared to devalue the senate's role in government, and to place their emphasis on manipulating the popular assemblies. The first notable *popularis* was Ti. Sempronius Gracchus (tribune of the plebs in 133 BC). Although the term fell into disuse after the republic, nobles of this view tended to identify with the Julian family of Augustus, perhaps reflecting Caesar's position of primacy among the *populares* in the 50s and 40s BC.

Praefectus: Under the principate, the term 'prefect' was applied to various grades within the reformed equestrian order, from the commands of auxiliary army units to some of the highest officers in the order – *praefecti* of Egypt and of the Praetorian Guard.

Praetor: This was the office second in importance to the consulship, although the *praetors* may in the earliest days have been the chief magistrates – *prae-itor* 'one who goes in front'. From Sulla's time they had an increasing importance as the presiding officers in the courts (*quaestiones*); the post led on to legionary commands and/or governorships of second-rank provinces.

Princeps: The term 'chief man' was favoured by Augustus as a form of address; it did not imply a particular office, but through the republic had been applied to those who, in or out of office, were deemed to be prestigious, influential and disposers of patronage. The honorific title *princeps iuventutis* ('leader of youth') was sometimes bestowed on young members of the imperial family – such as Gaius and Lucius Caesar, Tiberius Gemellus and Nero himself in AD 50.

Princeps senatus: A republican term applied to the man who in terms of seniority (however conceived) was placed at the head of the list of senators, as Augustus was after the *lectio senatus* of 28 BC.

Proconsul: The term was originally applied to a consul whose *imperium* had been extended beyond his term of office as consul to enable him to continue command of an army; by the second century BC it was regularly applied to those who commanded provinces after their year of office in Rome: during the principate it was used of the governors (whether ex-consuls or ex-praetors) of senatorial provinces.

Procurator: The term was used of various grades of equestrian in the emperor's financial service – from the chief agents in the provinces, down to quite minor officials in their departments. They were officially distinguished by an adjective describing their different salary levels (e.g. *procurator ducenarius*).

Respublica: This word, often used emotively to describe the nature of the state which Augustus supplanted after Actium, means simply 'the public concern'. By definition, therefore, it would be negated by anyone with overwhelming and capriciously exercised powers (*dominatio*).

Senatus consultum: The decree issued at the end of a senatorial debate which was not *legally* binding, but an advisory statement passing on the senate's opinion to those popular bodies responsible for making the final decisions and passing laws.

Tribune of the plebs: Originally appointed according to tradition in 494 BC, the tribunes were officers charged with defending their fellow plebeians against injustices perpetrated by patricians. The decisive elements in their 'armoury' were the 'veto' by which they could bring any business (except that of a dictator) to a halt, and the 'sacrosanctity', by which all plebeians were bound by oath to defend an injured or wronged tribune. Gradually, the tribunes were drawn into the regular business of office-holding – almost, but not quite, part of the *cursus honorum*; their veto was employed increasingly as a *factional* weapon, and they became potentially powerful through their ability to legislate with the plebeian assembly *without* prior consultation of the senate. Under the principate, little of their power remained, dominated as it was by the emperor's tribunician power (*tribunicia potestas*). Augustus, because he was by adoption a patrician, could not hold the *office* of tribune, though between 36 and 23 BC he acquired most of the office's elements and outwardly used them as the basis of his conduct of government in Rome. The power served to stress his patronage and protection of all plebeians.

Triumvirate: Any group of *three* men; the first triumvirate of 60 BC was the informal arrangement for mutual assistance between Pompey, Crassus and Caesar; the second triumvirate of 43 BC was the legally based 'office' of Octavian, Antony and Lepidus. The term continued to be used of occasional groups of three, and regularly of the three mint officials, *triumviri* [or *tresviri*] *monetales*, and the punishment officials, *triumviri* [or *tresviri*] *capitales*, both of which groups were sections of the board of twenty, or *vigintivirate*, the first posts on the senatorial *cursus honorum*.

APPENDIX IV

Accounts of Nero's life and principate

The Classical authors

The principal accounts of Nero's life and reign which survive from antiquity are to be found in Tacitus' *Annals* (Books XII–XVI, written *c.* AD 115–120), Suetonius' *Life of Nero* (written in the AD 120s) and Dio Cassius' *Roman History* (Books LXI–LXIII, written *c.* AD 220–225). Of these, only Suetonius' biography is complete; Tacitus' account breaks off in the middle of the events of AD 66, while Dio's exists only in the form provided by a group of Byzantine epitomators. In addition to these there are accounts of Nero's fall in both Suetonius' and Plutarch's biographies of his successor Galba (both written in the AD 120s), while the Jewish war of AD 67–73 is treated in considerable detail by the Jewish historian of the Flavian period, Flavius Josephus (*Jewish Wars*, Books II–IV).

With the exception of Josephus, who was himself a particip-ant in the Jewish war of Nero's reign, these sources were separated from Nero's time by a considerable period of years and were thus dependent upon sources which no longer survive. The accounts of Tacitus, Suetonius and Dio, while different in emphasis and coverage, have enough similarities even in word-ing to indicate their use of common sources; it is, however, thought unlikely that they have any substantial interdependence. Suetonius' denial of the allegation that Nero's poetry was plagiarized, which was based upon his own perusal of Nero's papers, may be one of very few instances in which a critical comment upon Tacitus is intended.

All our sources are strongly critical of Nero although Tacitus, in making a distinction between what preceded and what followed the murder of Agrippina in AD 59, does allow for deterioration as a progressive phenomenon. He alone of our sources does record versions of events that were more favourable to Nero – for example, his denial of the allegations concerning Nero's examination of his mother's corpse and his responsibility for the Great Fire; even the rebuilding programme is at least partly attributed to the ambitions of the architects, Severus and Celer, rather than to Nero personally.

Suetonius' account concentrates on anecdotal material – of which the Elder Pliny may have been a principal source – which was designed to show Nero in a poor light; further, he omits events such as the British and Armenian campaigns, in which Nero took no personal part. Dio Cassius' epitomators, as often, play the part of moralizing and sensationalizing detractors of the emperor.

Yet Josephus indicates that he knew of sources more favourable to Nero; it may be that Tacitus in part reflects them with his thesis of deterioration, which is evident also in Lucan's *Pharsalia*, the poem on the civil war between Pompey and Caesar. In the main, however, historical sources favourable to Nero were 'sanitized' during the Flavian period which remained universally hostile to the last of the Julio–Claudians.

Suetonius and Dio Cassius both indicate their use of sources, but do not name them; Tacitus, however, although not as conscientious about naming sources as he promised to be, does identify a number of writers whom he used. The chief of these were the Elder Pliny, Cluvius Rufus and Fabius Rusticus. The Elder Pliny died in the eruption of Vesuvius in AD 79; although his historical writing has not survived, we do have his *Natural History*, which has been identified as the source of some information found in Suetonius and in Dio Cassius. References in the *Natural History* suggest the author's hostility to Nero, while the composition of the work as a whole indicates its author as essentially a compiler who was not particularly critical in his selection of material.

Cluvius Rufus has often been regarded as Tacitus' principal source; he was a courtier of Nero's but was not regarded as responsible for any of the period's more vicious tendencies. He is known to have been critical of Verginius Rufus' stance in AD 68, which probably reflects Flavian approval of Vindex and Galba. By implication, a criticism of Verginius Rufus would indicate sympathy with the cause that destroyed Nero. Nonetheless, it may be that Cluvius Rufus entertained a little more sympathy for Nero than other writers; in this case, it is probably reasonable to recognize his influence upon Tacitus. Fabius Rusticus, who was still alive in Trajan's reign, was a pupil and client of Seneca, and is at one point criticized by Tacitus for his bias in Seneca's favour. His attachment to Seneca would presumably indicate hostility to Nero, although perhaps recognizing a progressive deterioration. We may assume that Fabius Rusticus would have needed to defend the worldly Seneca against the criticisms of more 'committed' stoics, who appear to have become more extreme in their anti-monarchic views as the Flavian period developed.

Many leading figures composed 'memoirs' and Tacitus indicates his use of those of Domitius Corbulo; he also cites – though not for Neronian events – a 'family memoir' composed by Nero's mother. In addition, Tacitus records his use of the senatorial chronicle (*acta senatus*) and the accounts of a number of those who survived Piso's conspiracy in AD 65. It is likely too that Tacitus consulted the growing body of stoic 'hagiography' composed during the Flavian period.

A few other works of the period survive, including a number of Seneca's philosophical treatises and his *Moral Letters*; while these shed much light on his character and views, the treatise 'On Clemency' (*De Clementia*) appears to have been of particular importance in its purpose of trying to appraise Nero of the duties and conduct of a *princeps*. An expression of contemporary stoic values is to be found in the erudite *Satires* of Persius. At the other end of the scale, the surviving portions of the *Satyricon*, written by Nero's friend and 'arbiter of elegance' Petronius, offer revealing insights into contemporary 'low life'.

The literary sources for Nero's reign are discussed briefly in the following:

K.R. Bradley, *Suetonius' Life of Nero, An Historical Commentary*, Brussels 1978.

M.T. Griffin, *Nero: The End of a Dynasty*, London 1984 (pp. 235–7).

R. Syme, *Tacitus*, Oxford 1958 (particularly Chapters III, V and VI).

B. Warmington, *Nero: Reality and Legend*, London 1969 (pp. 1–9).

Non-literary evidence

A number of important documents survive from Nero's principate; they can be found in collections, such as:

S.J. Miller, *Inscriptions of the Roman Empire,* AD *14–117*, London 1971 (*Lactor* No. 8).

E.M. Smallwood, *Documents Illustrating the Principates of Gaius, Claudius and Nero*, Cambridge 1967.

Nero's coinage has been shown to provide a valuable contribution to the study of his reign, particularly of the later years, when it carries clear indications of the emperor's growing megalomania. A number of events of the reign are alluded to – such as the opening of the rebuilt harbour at Ostia, the opening of the new market (*macellum*) and the securing of peace in the east. The coins of this period are generally regarded as having attained new heights of production quality. It should also be noted that the various coinages which appeared in provinces in the early months of AD 68 are of particular importance in attempts to elucidate the motives and allegiances of those involved. For discussions see:

D.W. MacDowell, *The Western Coinages of Nero*, New York 1979.

M.T. Griffin, *Nero: The End of a Dynasty*, London 1984 (pp. 238–9).

C.M. Kraay, The Coinage of Vindex and Galba, AD 68, *Numismatic Chronicle* IX (1949), 129–49.

C.H.V. Sutherland, *Coinage in Roman Imperial Policy, 31* BC–AD *68*, London 1951 (particularly Chapter VIII).

C.H.V. Sutherland, *The Emperor and the Coinage*, London 1976 (particularly Chapter V).
C.H.V. Sutherland, *The Roman Imperial Coinage*, vol. I (second edition), London 1984 (pp. 133–215).

Modern authorities

A considerable number of biographies and analyses of Nero's life and reign have appeared over the years, reflecting the continuing fascination with and interpretative difficulties associated with the last of the Julio–Claudians. The more significant of these are:

B.W. Henderson, *The Life and Principate of the Emperor Nero*, London 1903.
B.H. Warmington, *Nero: Reality and Legend*, London 1969.
M.T. Griffin, *Nero: The End of a Dynasty*, London 1984.

In addition, there are many studies of aspects and personalities of the reign –
A.A. Barrett, *Agrippina: Mother of Nero*, London 1996.
A. Boethius, *The Golden House of Nero*, Ann Arbor 1976.
P.A. Brunt, Stoicism and the Principate, *Papers of the British School at Rome* XLII (1975), 7–35.
R.J. Fears, The Solar Monarchy of Nero and the Imperial Panegyric of Q. Curtius Rufus, *Historia* XXV (1976), 494–6.
M.T. Griffin, *Seneca: A Philosopher in Politics*, Oxford 1976.
B. Levick, *Claudius*, London 1990.
T.K. Roper, Nero, Seneca and Tigellinus, *Historia* XXVIII (1979), 346–57.
V. Rudich, *Political Dissidence under Nero*, London 1992.
R. Syme, Domitius Corbulo, *Journal of Roman Studies* LX (1970), 27–39.
R. Syme, Partisans of Galba, *Historia* XXXI (1982), 460–83.
T. Wiedemann, *The Julio–Claudian Emperors*, London 1989.

The rebellion of Vindex and the fall of Nero has in itself produced an extensive bibliography, such as:

P.A. Brunt, The Revolt of Vindex and the Fall of Nero, *Latomus* XVIII (1959), 531–59.

G.E.F. Chilver, The Army in Politics, *Journal of Roman Studies* XLVII (1957), 29–35.

J.B. Hainsworth, Verginius and Vindex, *Historia* XI (1962), 86–96.

C. Murison, *Galba, Otho and Vitellius: Careers and Controversies*, Hildesheim 1993 (particularly Chapter 1).

D.C.A. Shotter, Tacitus and Verginius Rufus, *Classical Quarterly* XVII (1967), 370–81.

D.C.A. Shotter, A Timetable for the *Bellum Neronis*, *Historia* XXIV (1975), 59–74.

The year of the four emperors is recounted and its problems discussed in:

K. Wellesley, *The Long Year*, AD 69, Bristol 1989 (second edition).